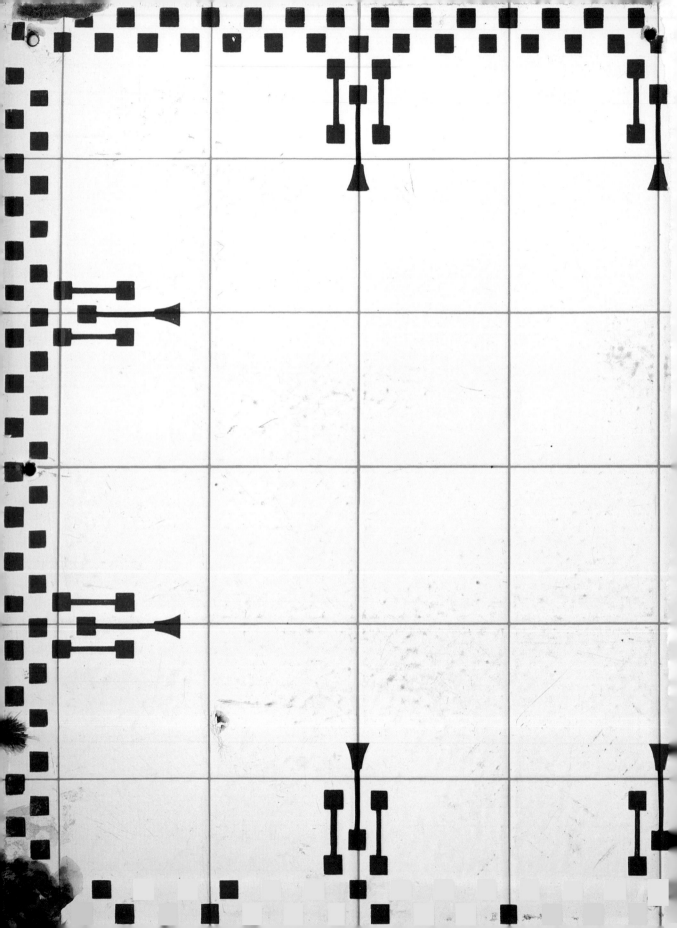

THE
ARTISAN
MARKET

THE ARTISAN MARKET

EMMA MACDONALD

DUNCAN BAIRD PUBLISHERS

LONDON

To my parents for the delicious meals they prepared for us as children, and their early inspiration and encouragement to follow my passion for food. And more latterly to my husband and three wonderful sons who regularly endure experimental suppers and assist me in making endless batches of soups and preserves.

The Artisan Market
Emma Macdonald

Distributed in the USA and Canada by
Sterling Publishing Co., Inc.
387 Park Avenue South
New York, NY 10016-8810

First published in the UK and USA in 2013 by
Duncan Baird Publishers, an imprint of
Watkins Publishing Limited
Sixth Floor
75 Wells Street
London W1T 3QH

A member of Osprey Group

Managing Editor: Grace Cheetham
Editor: Emma Clegg
Recipe Tester: Nicola Graimes
Americanizers: Beverly LeBlanc and Norma MacMillan
Managing Designer: Suzanne Tuhrim
Commissioned photography: Toby Scott, except on pages 69, 70, 129, 173 and 219 by William Lingwood
Food Stylist: Jayne Cross, except on pages 69, 70, 129, 173 and 219 by Bridget Sargeson
Prop Stylist: Lucy Harvey
Commissioned artwork: Jade Wheaton
Picture Research: Emma Copestake
Production: Uzma Taj

ISBN: 978-1-84899-115-6

1 3 5 7 9 10 8 6 4 2

Typeset in Du Turner and Rockwell
Color reproduction by PDQ, UK
Printed in China

For information about custom editions, special sales, premium and corporate purchases, please contact
Sterling Special Sales Department at 800-805-5489 or specialsales@sterlingpub.com.

Notes on the Recipes
Unless otherwise stated:
Use large eggs
Use medium fruit and vegetables
Use fresh ingredients, including herbs and chilies
1 tsp. = 5ml   1 tbsp. =15ml   1 cup = 240ml

Publisher's note: While every care has been taken in compiling the recipes for this book, Watkins Publishing Limited, or any other persons who have been involved in working on this publication, cannot accept responsibility for any errors or omissions, inadvertent or not, that may be found in the recipes or text, nor for any problems that may arise as a result of preparing one of these recipes. If you are pregnant or breastfeeding or have any special dietary requirements or medical conditions, it is advisable to consult a medical professional before following any of the recipes contained in this book.

Contents

6 Foreword
7 Cooking the Bay Tree Way

1. MEAT & POULTRY
16 Light Meals
28 Main Meals

2. FISH & SHELLFISH
46 Light Meals
58 Main Meals

3. CHEESE & DAIRY
74 Light Meals
88 Main Meals

4. DRESSINGS, RUBS & SAUCES
104 Light Meals
116 Main Meals

5. VEGETABLES
132 Light Meals
146 Main Meals

6. FRUIT
162 Light Meals
168 Main Meals
176 Desserts

7. BAKED GOODS
192 Crackers & Bread
204 Cookies, Cakes & Desserts

220 Index
224 Acknowledgments

FOREWORD

After almost twenty years in the food business, a great wish of mine has been to publish my own cookbook —and now here it is, *The Artisan Market*, a collection of my favorite deli secrets, and so much more.

From the age of thirteen I wanted to make a career in cooking and I spent much of my free time devising new recipes and baking cakes for friends and family. I studied catering in college and, after finishing, I worked as an apprentice in a number of restaurants in France before traveling through Asia, working in various restaurants and catering establishments as I went. This was a great way of learning to appreciate different cultures, ingredients and styles of cooking. In Asia, I discovered the eclectic mix of spices sold in markets and how they are used in cooking, along with the techniques that make Asian cuisines so fresh and vibrant. This has influenced my own style of cooking, especially in the way I like to add a fresh interpretation to classic recipes in our Bay Tree condiments.

I grew up in a house where there was always a supply of homemade jams and chutneys, so it seemed a natural progression to start making my own, and, in time, I decided to make a living from it. I established The Bay Tree Food Co. in my early twenties, producing traditional, home-cooked condiments and marmalades with a modern twist. More recently, we have moved into creating home-style ready-made sauces and pasta sauces. One of our greatest early successes was AGA-dried tomatoes, but, unfortunately, the demand far outweighed the volume we could make at the time. So we then set our sights on what could be done without sacrificing our desire to create high-quality products without any artificial additives.

It hasn't always been plain sailing, and I quickly found that making products in a jar with a good shelf life (as opposed to making a meal to be eaten right away) requires a certain amount of food science, but this aspect has also always fascinated me. Recognizing and appreciating that fresh produce can vary in taste, texture or color, depending on the season, weather and growing conditions, and using this knowledge, can make such a big difference to the end product. I always aim to make products as close as I can to the home-cooked equivalent without compromising on flavor and texture, or having to add artificial additives, while also offering the convenience of a product with a good shelf life.

The recipes in this book—like The Bay Tree products—are predominantly based on a traditional theme, but with an exciting twist. My recipe for gravlax (see page 56), for example, features fresh lemon and gingerroot to flavor the salmon, instead of the more classic dill. I also hope you'll try making pâtés, preserves, sauces and even some home-smoking. If this doesn't appeal to you, there are also recipes that use these ingredients bought already prepared from a deli for those times when you want to make a mouthwatering meal quickly. Some recipes are simple and others demand more effort, but either way the end results are worth it!

I've also included recipes for some of our popular Bay Tree products, such as Piccalilli (see page 138), which is adapted from a traditional recipe but with a little extra something to perk it up. While piccalilli is excellent served with a meat or cheese platter, I also wanted to show how it can be used as part of a meal, in this case rémoulade (see page 139). You can also create this recipe with a store-bought piccalilli. Homemade condiments, jams and sauces are such a treat to have in the kitchen and are a delight to give to family and friends. The fact that they are so appreciated and enjoyed makes the effort more than worthwhile.

I hope you'll enjoy these recipes and find the time to be creative making your own deli products, as well as using the ready-made ones in the recipes.

COOKING THE BAY TREE WAY

A good deli is a fantastic treasure trove of culinary delights, from cured meats, smoked fish and sweet preserves to artisan cheeses, fresh pasta and hand-crafted savory pies.

This book is designed to be both accessible and inspiring, featuring a collection of recipes for dishes that incorporate deli foods you buy and also more challenging recipes, showing how you can create your own deli products at home, such as home-cured bacon, ricotta cheese, fresh pasta, flavored vinegar, seafood pâté and artisan breads. There are also suggestions for how to give classic deli foods an interesting new spin, such as a crab terrine that forms the filling of a creamy seafood tart (see page 49), or a recipe for home-smoked chicken breasts that gives a delicious subtle smokiness to a classic paella (see page 29), or a garlic and fennel mustard that makes a flavorsome crust for a roasted leg of lamb (see page 123). Whether you buy your deli products or make them from scratch, there's a wonderful variety to choose from.

MEAT & POULTRY

While the French term "charcuterie" might traditionally have meant pork products, it has become a generic word encompassing all manner of cured and preserved meats from all over the world. Pork still reigns supreme in the world of charcuterie, however, thanks to its incredible versatility: just think pâtés, terrines, bacon, salami, sausages, ham and savory pies.

Arguably the finest and most expensive ham is the Spanish jamón Ibérico. The Ibérico pig roams freely and spends its final months in oak forests feeding on acorns (bellota), which give the meat a unique delicate, sweet flavor. The curing process that follows takes at least twelve months and up to thirty-six months, to produce a ham with melt-in-the-mouth qualities. Salt-curing draws out the moisture in meat, thus intensifying the flavor and firming up the texture. It also inhibits the growth of harmful bacteria. You can try salt-curing with the recipe for Home-Cured Bacon (see page 22), which is immensely satisfying and rewarding to make.

Game—both feathered and furred—is becoming more widely available and is enjoying a resurgence in popularity. Rabbit, pheasant, partridge, squab pigeon and venison are perfect for savory pies, pâtés, terrines and potted meats, but because they are low in fat you usually need to combine them with a fattier meat, such as duck or pork, to keep them moist. It's the generous fat content that makes duck and pork perfect for rillettes, potted meat, confit and pâtés. When you're making meat pâtés, try duck, goose and chicken livers, which are not expensive to buy and create a great base flavor.

FISH & SHELLFISH

Fish and shellfish can be smoked, salted, cured or pickled, but if you intend to preserve your own seafood, the key is to use the freshest you can buy.

Home-smoking is growing in popularity. Home-Smoked Trout (see page 68) is easy to make so is a great starting point. The fish is hot-smoked, which cooks it while imparting a delicate smokiness. You don't need any special equipment; I use an old wok, but a sturdy cracker tin, or galvanized garbage pan if smoking on a larger scale outdoors, work well, or you can invest in a purpose-built hot-smoker.

In contrast, cold-smoking is a much longer, slower process. It does not cook the food, but gives it a much more intense smokiness than hot-smoking, and it also extends the shelf life of the fish, which is cured before smoking. Cold-smoking requires investment in specialist large pieces of smoking equipment, so is probably out of the scope of most home cooks. But cold-smoked fish is widely sold. Salmon is probably the most popular cold-smoked fish, but look for sturgeon and mackerel, too, both of which are delicious when sliced very thinly and served on rye bread with pickled cucumber or a spoonful of cucumber relish, or with blinis and sour cream or crème fraîche. Other smoky delights include smoked mussels and oysters, herring (kippers) and eel.

Herring and mackerel that have been pickled, brined, marinated or soused (cooked or raw fish that has been soaked in a flavored light white wine or vinegar marinade-cum-dressing) are a familiar sight on deli counters and are also sold in jars. They make very tasty canapés, or they can be enjoyed as a flavorsome light lunch served on Scandinavian crispbread with a dill potato salad, or cut into paper-thin slices and served with a mustard-flavored mayonnaise and a crisp green salad.

When it comes to anchovies, we tend to love them or hate them! This small fish, belonging to the herring family, is sold in many forms: whole, filleted, salted, brined, in oil, in vinegar and/or flavored with chilies, spices or herbs. If you want to tame any saltiness, first soak the anchovies in milk or water and then pat them dry. Usually found on top of pizzas or in a salade Niçoise, anchovies are also used to make numerous types of a sauce-cum-dip, including the gutsy French anchoïade, the Italian bagna cauda, the Provençal tapenade and the quintessentially English *Patum Peperium*, or Gentleman's Relish.

DAIRY & CHEESE

Milk is at the heart of all things dairy, whether from a cow, sheep or goat (or buffalo), and it is incredibly versatile. Yogurt is a cultured milk product that is a common ingredient in both cooked and uncooked dishes. I like to use a lighter, fresher yogurt in Indian raitas and salad dressings or in baking, reserving the richer, creamier alternatives, particularly Greek yogurt made from sheep's milk, for sauces or desserts.

Cream also comes in many guises. Light cream is great for pouring over desserts or fruit salads, while heavy or heavy whipping cream is the one to use for cooking, because it is less likely to split when heated due to its higher fat content. Heavy cream can be whipped thick too, so is perfect for filling cakes and pastries and for dolloping on fruit pies and desserts. For the best results when whipping cream, always make sure the cream, bowl and beaters are chill-cold before you start.

This book includes recipes for Labneh (see page 78) and a Rich Homemade Ricotta (see page 218). These fresh, mild cheeses are a great starting point for making your own cheeses at home and it's worth experimenting with them by adding different herbs and spices.

The next step on from making fresh cheese is to add rennet, which encourages milk to separate into curds and whey; after this separation process, the curds are salted and pressed, then left to mature or ripen. This is, of course, an ultra-simplistic description of how this wonderful food product is made, and there are many thousands of different types of cheese, each with its own nuances, which are influenced not only by the cheesemaking process but also by the source of the milk.

When you're serving cheese, whichever type you choose, it is always best to let it come to room temperature, so the flavor can develop and come to the fore, and the texture can become more yielding.

CUPBOARD CONDIMENTS

A well-stocked kitchen cupboard, or pantry, is a wondrous thing. Shelves laden with oils, vinegars, sauces, dressings, preserves, pastes, herbs and spices not only look appealing, but are fundamental to the success of so many dishes. A spoonful of spice paste or a splash of chili oil, for example, can transform a dish into something special. To keep all your pantry ingredients in tip-top condition, be sure to store the jars in a cool, dry and dark place until you open them.

My pantry cupboard houses a huge range of vinegars: balsamic, red and white wine, rice wine, apple cider and malt vinegar—all of which can be used on their own or as part of a preserve. Fresh relishes and flavored vinegars benefit from being made with good-quality wine vinegar or apple cider vinegar, while you can get away with a more economical and robust malt vinegar in strongly flavored chutneys. Use a vinegar that is at least 5 percent acid (this is normally indicated on the label), because homemade preserves should have a low pH or high acidity if they are to last for any length of time.

I also have a good selection of oils: an extra virgin olive oil (essential), plus a lighter olive oil for cooking; a toasted sesame oil for Asian dishes; a good-quality canola or grapeseed oil; and a small bottle of truffle oil, a splash of which can transform many dishes. I also like to make my own flavored oils using herbs, chilies, spices and citrus zests. I've found that using organically grown herbs gives the best flavor, and recommend using zest from unwaxed citrus fruit.

Flavored oils are best made in small quantities, because they will deteriorate, and I advise storing them in the refrigerator and using within a few weeks. If flavored oils become too warm, there is a risk that they will become rancid, and there is also a low, but possible, risk of spoilage caused by molds and the bacterium *Clostridium botulinum* (botulism). This is because you are preserving an ingredient in a low-acid environment, without heating it to boiling point first (which would kill off many unwanted bacteria). You need to be particularly careful when flavoring oils with fresh garlic or fresh chili.

Garlic-flavored oil is best used within a few days of making (keep it in the refrigerator); for longer storage—up to a month—roast or blanch the garlic first. Similarly, chilies should be roasted or blanched, or you can use dried chilies. Dried herbs and spices are a good and possibly safer alternative to fresh, and make flavored oils with a longer shelf life.

FRUIT & VEGETABLES

Fruit can be canned whole in sugar syrup or alcohol, or it can be cooked down to make jam or jelly. Both fruits and vegetables can be pickled or made into a chutney or relish to add spice to cold cuts, cheese and sandwiches. Preserving, or "putting by," is a perfect method for using up a glut of fruit or vegetables, but bear in mind that top-quality fresh produce will make the best-quality preserve. Damaged, bruised and soft specimens are usually best avoided.

When making jam it's preferable to use fruit that is slightly underripe, because it has a higher acidity level, as well as more pectin, both of which will help the jam to set. It's not necessary to make a large quantity—in fact, even a pint of strawberries is sufficient to make a jar of jam in little more than 10 minutes. If you intend to keep a jam or other sweet preserve for any length of time you need to use a sufficient amount of sugar and cook it at a high temperature (180°F). Made this way, sweet preserves should keep for up to two years if stored in a cool, dry, dark place; once opened, they should be refrigerated and eaten within a few months.

Fruit and vegetable chutneys and relishes not only make great condiments, but a spoonful can also add extra "oomph" to stews, sauces and curries. In addition to fruit and/or vegetables, a chutney needs a combination of sugar, vinegar and salt, added in the right proportions. Together these enable the chutney to keep well, giving the flavors time to mature. Spices also act as a preservative: coriander, cumin and mustard seeds, star anise, nutmeg, cardamom, juniper and dried chilies all will enhance a chutney's flavor.

There doesn't seem to be a lot of difference between a chutney and a relish—both are mixtures of chopped (coarsely or finely) fruit and vegetables simmered with vinegar, sugar and flavorings until thickened. The texture of a chutney or relish may be chunky or smooth, and flavors of both range from sweet to sour and spicy. Pickles, though, while very similar in using a seasoned vinegar or brine mixture, are made with whole or large pieces of fruit and vegetables, and the resulting texture is firmer and crisper. Vegetables and fruit often pickled include cucumber, onions, beets, cauliflower, baby corn, red cabbage, pears, apples and watermelon rind. Those vegetables with a high water content, such as cucumbers and zucchini, need to be brined or dry-salted before pickling to remove excess water.

HOW TO STERILIZE JARS

There is nothing more satisfying and rewarding than making your own preserved foods. With all types of preserving, paying careful attention to hygiene and safety is paramount, but it's all pretty straightforward if you stick to the guidelines here.

Thickened glass canning jars are suitable for most preserves. It is essential to sterilize them before use by washing in hot soapy water, then rinsing well in scalding water. Closures such as screwbands and lids also need to be sterilized in this way, or according to the manufacturer's directions. If your preserves are not going to be processed in a boiling-water bath (see below), the jars and closures need further sterilization: set them on a rack in a large pan of water (they should be totally submerged), bring to a boil and boil for 15 minutes. Remove from the heat, but leave the jars in the hot water until you are going to fill them.

For Mason jars with two-piece screwband metal lids, always use new lids. The screwbands can be used again though, unless they're rusted, bent or otherwise damaged. You can buy packs of lids (and screwbands) in various sizes from kitchen shops and online. Jar rubbers also need to be replaced each time. Before use, wash them in hot soapy water and rinse with very hot water (don't boil them).

Whatever type of canning jar you use, be sure it has no cracks, chips or scratches and that the sealing rims are perfectly smooth. If your jars have glass lids, these too must have smooth, chip-free edges. And don't use old jars for which you cannot get suitable new closures.

PACKING & STORING

Always pack a hot jam, jelly, relish or other preserve into a hot jar. If the jar has not been kept hot after sterilization, it needs to be warmed again, because pouring boiling hot preserves into a cooled jar could cause the jar to shatter. (In my experience, this is rare and generally only happens if there is a fault in the glass that isn't visible, but it is best to be cautious.) Raw food to be canned, such as vegetables to be pickled or whole fruit, should also be packed into hot jars, then covered with hot vinegar solution or syrup.

1 Fill each jar to within ½ inch of the rim (if you are going to process your preserves in a water bath, you need to leave more space or "headroom"). Then run a sterilized slender rubber or plastic spatula (not metal) down through the contents of the jar to release any pockets of trapped air.
2 Wipe the rim of the jar with paper towel, then put on the sterilized closure tightly, or according to the directions for the type of canning jars you are using.
3 If you are going to process in a water bath (see below), set each jar in the kettle as soon as it has been filled and capped. Once the jars are cool, check the seals, if necessary, then wipe the jars clean and label them, making a note of the contents and the date.

To ensure that your preserves have a good shelf life, it makes sense to "process" the jars in a boiling-water bath. The kettle you use can be a special water-bath canner or a big stockpot with a rack in the bottom.

The kettle needs to be deep enough so the jars can be covered by 1 to 2 inches of boiling water. Half fill the kettle with water and start heating it. As the jars are filled, set them on the rack so they are not touching the side of the kettle or each other (note that jars of raw food should not be put into boiling water, which could make them crack). Pour more hot water down the side of the kettle so the jars are covered, then bring to a boil and process for the required time. Remove and let cool overnight.

Store your preserves in a cool, dark, dry place, and then in the refrigerator after opening. Many chutneys, relishes and pickles benefit from a period of maturation, during which the flavor develops and mellows. They might darken in color, too, but this should not be a cause for alarm if the preserves have been made and packed using the guidelines given above.

EQUIPMENT

A **jelly** or **candy thermometer** is a boon when making jelly, jam and marmalade. It helps you test for doneness, to guarantee that your preserves will set. It also ensures that they will keep well without spoilage.

Bacteria is most active between 50°F and 120°F, and while chilling or freezing restrains activity, these processes don't kill them. Boiling at 180°F, however, kills most yeasts and molds, but not spore-forming bacteria that can be controlled in most cases by acidity and sugar concentration. If you want to get serious about the process of preserving, a **digital pH meter** is also useful. This will allow you to check your preserve's acidity, which can help to get a better set in jams and, with a bit of knowledge, to ascertain its potential shelf life.

An **enameled or stainless steel kettle** with a thick, heavy bottom will keep your jam, marmalade or jelly at a rolling boil without it sticking. Some, designed for preserving, have graduated marks on the side to make it easy to see how much liquid has evaporated. Avoid using aluminum pans, because they will taint the flavor of your preserve. A **wide-mouth funnel** is useful for filling jars without spills, but make sure you sterilize it first.

One of the most useful pieces of equipment in my kitchen is my **immersion blender**, because using it, rather than a food processor or regular blender, is a convenient and simple way of pureeing fruit and vegetables, and making mayonnaise, batters, bread crumbs and dressings.

RECIPES TO TREASURE

Today, no deli would be worth its weight in gold without an inspirational and mouthwatering selection of delicious goodies, from a cave-ripened Roquefort and layered seafood terrine to a hot-water-crust savory pork pie and exquisite fruit-packed preserves. I hope that my collection of recipes in this book will be equally inspiring, and that they prove to be as much a feast for the eyes as for the tastebuds.

1. Meat
&
Poultry

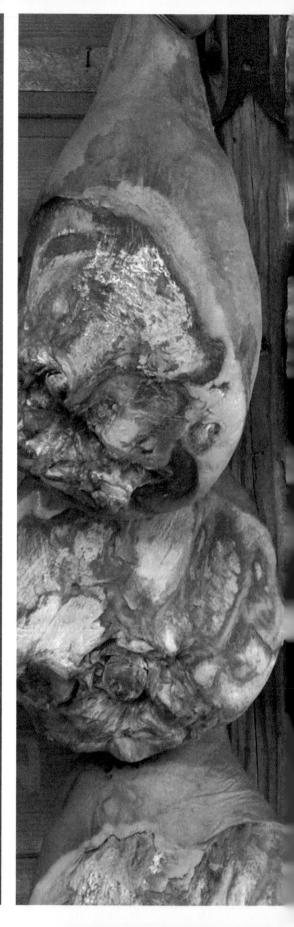

Duck Rillettes

Making rillettes is a good way of preserving meat. In this recipe, the duck is slow-roasted first to render the fat, which is then used for packing the rillettes and to give the meat a great depth of flavor. Depending on how fatty your duck legs are, you might not be able to use them to create enough extra fat, in which case you can buy additional duck or goose fat. The rillettes will keep for up to 2 weeks in the refrigerator.

**SERVES 6   PREPARATION TIME: 30 MINUTES, PLUS COOLING AND INFUSING
COOKING TIME: 2 HOURS 10 MINUTES**

2 teaspoons sea salt, plus extra to taste
¼ teaspoon freshly ground black pepper, plus extra to taste
½ teaspoon Chinese five-spice powder or apple pie spice
4 good-size, fatty duck legs
7 tablespoons white wine
2 star anise
2 garlic cloves, sliced
about 7 tablespoons duck or goose fat (as needed)
toast or crackers and a green salad, to serve

Heat the oven to 300°F. Mix together the salt, pepper and Chinese five spice. Rub the spice mixture all over the flesh side of the duck legs.

Put the duck legs, skin-side up, in a tight-fitting roasting pan. Spoon any leftover spices over the duck. Pour 2 tablespoons water into the pan, cover tightly with foil so the duck cooks in its own fat and roast for 2 hours, or until the meat is almost falling off the bone but is still moist. Remove the pan from the oven and leave the duck legs to cool completely, still covered with foil.

Remove the duck legs from the roasting pan and scrape off any cooking fat into a small pan. Discard the skin and bones and transfer all the duck meat into a bowl. Shred the meat into rough strips using your hands or two forks.

Put the wine, star anise and garlic in a saucepan and bring to a boil. Let the wine bubble away until it reduces by three-quarters, then add the fat from the duck and any juices left in the pan. You need to have sufficient fat to cover the duck to preserve it. If you don't have enough fat from the roasted duck at this point, add extra duck or goose fat. Return to a boil, then remove from the heat, season to taste with salt and plenty of pepper and leave for 30 minutes so the flavors infuse.

Remove the garlic and star anise with a slotted spoon, then pour the mixture over the shredded duck. Pack the duck into six large ramekins or a single terrine. Leave to cool, then chill, covered, until ready to serve. Serve with toast or crackers and a green leaf salad, or use in the Chinese Pancakes with Crisp Duck Rillettes recipe on the facing page.

CHINESE PANCAKES WITH CRISP
DUCK RILLETTES

In this recipe, Duck Rillettes (see facing page) are used to make an excellent alternative to the traditional Chinese Peking duck, but unlike the classic Beijing dish, you use just the meat, rather than a combination of meat and skin. Purists will not be disappointed, however, because the crisp duck is served with all the usual accompaniments.

SERVES 4   PREPARATION TIME: 15 MINUTES   COOKING TIME: 15 MINUTES

1 recipe quantity Duck Rillettes
  (see facing page)
½ English cucumber, sliced lengthwise,
  seeded and cut into thin strips

4 scallions, shredded
4 tablespoons hoisin sauce or Chinese
  Plum Sauce (see page 121)
16 Chinese pancakes

Scrape off as much fat as possible from the duck rillettes. Heat a wok over high heat. Add half the duck rillettes, turn down the heat slightly and stir-fry for 5 minutes, or until crisp. Using a slotted spoon, remove the rillettes from the wok and drain on paper towels, then cover with foil and keep warm until ready to serve. Repeat with the remaining duck rillettes.

Put the cucumber, scallions and hoisin sauce in three separate dishes, ready to serve.

Steam the pancakes in two batches for a few minutes until warmed through. Wrap the first batch of pancakes in foil to keep them warm while you cook the second batch.

To serve, allow everyone to help themselves, rolling up the duck, cucumber and scallions in the pancakes and dipping them in the hoisin sauce before eating.

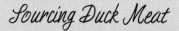

Sourcing Duck Meat

If you can, buy a wild or a free-range duck as it will have been naturally reared to higher welfare standards than an intensively bred bird. Ideally, ducks should be fed naturally, given access to ponds in an outdoor environment and allowed to grow slowly—this creates a happy bird and the best-flavored meat. The most common American breeds are Long Island and Peking. Choose a plump bird (or breast or legs if buying duck pieces) with skin that is smooth, dry and soft. The duck should not smell strong or be slimy.

GAME, CHICKEN & APRICOT PIE

This "raised" pie has a hot-water-pastry crust. Contrary to the normal rules of piecrust-making where all the ingredients and the dough should be kept as cool as possible, this dough is used while still warm. It is made by melting fat in liquid and bringing to a boil before beating in the flour. It is a substantial dough, perfect for encasing tall, freestanding pies without collapsing. I like to serve the pie with new potatoes and a green salad, but it's also great for a picnic.

SERVES 8 TO 10   PREPARATION TIME: 30 MINUTES, PLUS COOLING
COOKING TIME: 2 HOURS 20 MINUTES

FILLING:
3 tablespoons butter
4 shallots, finely chopped
2 garlic cloves, finely chopped
1¼ pounds boneless pork picnic
   shoulder, cubed
5 ounces bacon slices, finely chopped
1 teaspoon dried thyme
1 tablespoon chopped sage
1 to 2 teaspoons ground allspice
1 teaspoon juniper berries, crushed
2 tablespoons brandy
8 ounces boneless, skinless pheasant,
   sliced

⅔ cup dried apricots, halved crosswise
8 ounces boneless, skinless chicken
   thighs, sliced
sea salt and freshly ground black pepper

PASTRY DOUGH:
¾ cup lard, plus extra for greasing
7 tablespoons milk
2 eggs
4¼ cups all-purpose flour, plus extra
   for dusting
1 teaspoon salt

To make the filling, melt the butter in a large skillet over medium heat and fry the shallots and garlic for 5 minutes, or until soft. Transfer them to a bowl and leave to cool.

Grind the pork in a food processor, then transfer to a large bowl. Add the bacon, thyme, sage, allspice, juniper berries, brandy and cooled shallots and garlic. Season to taste with salt and pepper and stir until combined. (Check the seasoning by frying a little nugget of the mixture.) Leave to one side.

Heat the oven to 400°F. Grease a deep 8-inch springform pan with lard and line the bottom and side with parchment paper.

To make the dough, put ⅓ cup water in a saucepan with the milk and lard and bring to a boil, stirring until combined. Meanwhile, lightly beat 1 of the eggs. Mix together the flour and salt in a mixing bowl, make a central well and pour in the beaten egg and the hot lard mixture. Beat together with a wooden spoon until you have a smooth dough.

Turn the dough onto a lightly floured countertop and, when cool enough to handle, knead briefly. Cut off one-third of the dough and wrap in plastic wrap to keep it warm. Roll out the remaining warm dough on the lightly floured surface and use to line the bottom and side of the pan. The dough has a tendency to pull itself down, but persevere and patch any holes or cracks.

CONTINUED ON PAGE **20**

Spoon half of the ground pork mixture into the dough-lined pan. Add a layer of pheasant, then layers of apricots and chicken. Top with the remaining ground pork mixture, pressing down to make an even layer.

Lightly beat the remaining egg. Roll out the reserved dough into a circle on the lightly floured countertop. Brush the top of the dough edge in the pan with beaten egg and top with the dough circle. Trim the dough lid and pinch the edges together to seal securely. Brush the top of the pie with egg, then cut a ½-inch hole in the middle. Cut out shapes from the dough trimmings to decorate, then secure them on the lid with a little egg and brush with more egg.

Bake the pie for 20 minutes, then reduce the oven temperature to 325°F. Cover the top with foil to prevent it from browning too much and bake for 1¾ hours longer, or until golden brown.

Remove the pie from the oven and remove the side of the pan. Carefully put the pie on a cookie sheet, brush the side with beaten egg and bake for 10 minutes longer, or until golden. Remove from the oven and insert a skewer into the top of the pie: if the juices run clear, the pie is baked through. Leave it to cool on a wire rack for 10 minutes, then remove the pan bottom and the paper and leave to cool completely on the rack. The pie will keep in the refrigerator for up to 5 days.

COOK'S TIPS
• If the dough is too fragile when you first roll it out, simply re-form it into a ball, leave for a moment and then roll again. Don't let the dough become cold, however, because it will be difficult to use, becoming stiff and crumbly.
• Some bakers recommend using both butter and lard to make hot-water pastry dough for a slightly richer flavor, so you can replace 3 tablespoons of the lard with the same quantity of butter, if preferred.

Choosing Game

Pheasant is used here, but other choices are partridge, rabbit or venison. Prices vary, depending on the season and whether you are buying fresh or frozen meat. Buy game from a reliable source, who can tell you its provenance, how to prepare it and offer cooking advice.

Game is largely interchangeable in dishes such as pies, pâtés and potted meat. Because it is low in fat, it should be cooked gently for the best flavor and texture, usually with added fat to prevent it from drying out. In this pie, for example, the slices of pheasant are sandwiched between layers of ground pork, which has a higher fat content, to keep it moist and tender.

The flavor of game varies depending on the breed, feed and how it is matured or hung. Pheasant, like partridge, tends to have a mild flavor, a little stronger than chicken. Hen pheasants have a more subtle flavor than cocks, but have plumper breasts and more meat.

PASTRAMI WITH SWEET CUCUMBER RELISH ON RYE

An adaptation of the New York deli classic, this open-face sandwich comes with a fresh cucumber relish instead of the usual gherkins. Pastrami is cured, dried beef and is best served in thin slices.

SERVES 4   PREPARATION TIME: 20 MINUTES, PLUS SALTING   COOKING TIME: 3 MINUTES

2 tablespoons mayonnaise
1 teaspoon prepared English mustard
8 slices light rye bread
16 slices pastrami

SWEET CUCUMBER RELISH:
1 small English cucumber, ends trimmed
3 tablespoons good-quality white wine
   vinegar or rice wine vinegar
3 tablespoons sugar
1 tablespoon chopped dill
sea salt

To make the sweet cucumber relish, using a vegetable peeler or mandolin, cut the cucumber into long, thin slices. Put them in a colander and cover with sea salt. Leave to drain for 20 minutes, then rinse off the salt and pat dry with paper towels.

Meanwhile, heat the broiler. Mix together the mayonnaise and English mustard and leave to one side.

Mix together the vinegar and sugar in a nonmetallic bowl large enough to hold the cucumber. When the sugar has dissolved, add the cucumber and dill and turn in the vinegar mixture until coated.

Arrange the rye bread slices on the broiler rack and lightly toast on both sides. Spread each slice of toast with a little of the mustard mayonnaise, then top with 2 slices of pastrami. Drain the cucumber and lay it in folds on top of the pastrami.

Home-Cured Bacon

For the most superior bacon, use a pork belly with distinct layers of fat and meat, preferably from a heritage breed. If you can't find smoked salt, increase the coarse sea salt. Cut the bacon thickly for lardons or thinly for frying for breakfast.

MAKES ABOUT 1 POUND 5 OUNCES   PREPARATION TIME: ABOUT 5 DAYS

1 pound 5 ounces boneless fresh pork belly
4 tablespoons coarse sea salt
1 tablespoon smoked salt
1 tablespoon honey
1 tablespoon light brown sugar

Pat dry the pork belly all over and remove the rind, if you like. Mix together both types of salt, the honey and sugar in a nonmetallic bowl. Rub the mixture over both sides of the pork until it is completely covered. Put the pork in a thick ziplock plastic bag and expel as much air as possible, then seal. Put the bag on a plate and prop up one end so any liquid released from the pork runs away to the side.

Place in the refrigerator and leave for 3 days. Each day, pour off any liquid, reseal and return to the refrigerator. After 3 days, rinse the salt off the pork and pat it dry. (To check the flavor, cut off a small piece and fry it; if the bacon is too salty for your taste, soak it for 1 hour in water, then pat dry again.)

Put a rack inside a deep plastic, glass or ceramic dish. Put the pork on top and leave it in a cool, well-ventilated place for 2 days, covered with a piece of clean cheesecloth. Remove the bacon from the dish, wrap in wax paper and store in the refrigerator until ready to eat. A 5-day cure gives a lightly salted bacon, which will keep for up to 1 month, or it can be frozen for up to 3 months.

BACON, NECTARINE & GINGER SALAD

The combination of crisp, salty bacon and sweet, juicy nectarine with the heat from the preserved ginger is a real winner in this salad. It is dressed simply with lemon juice and extra virgin olive oil, which enhance the flavors of the main ingredients.

SERVES 4   PREPARATION TIME: 10 MINUTES   COOKING TIME: 7 MINUTES

8 thin slices Home-Cured Bacon
(see facing page)
2 balls preserved ginger in syrup, diced,
plus 2 tablespoons of the syrup
3 ounces mixed young salad greens
3 ounces pea shoots
2 ripe nectarines, halved, pitted and
sliced lengthwise

DRESSING:
4 tablespoons extra virgin olive oil,
preferably a fruity-flavored oil
2 tablespoons lemon juice
sea salt and freshly ground black pepper

Heat the broiler and line the broiler pan with foil. Broil the bacon for 5 minutes, turning once. Brush one side with the ginger syrup and broil for 1 minute longer, then turn the bacon over and repeat until crisp and golden brown. Leave to cool slightly, then break into large bite-size pieces.

Meanwhile, mix together all the ingredients for the dressing, seasoning to taste with salt and pepper.

Divide the salad greens and pea shoots among 4 serving bowls and top with the nectarines and preserved ginger. Spoon as much of the dressing over as needed, then toss gently until lightly coated. Scatter the bacon pieces over the top and serve.

QUAIL SCOTCH EGGS

These Scotch eggs are so satisfying to make and just the perfect size—great for a summer party, picnic or snack. Use good-quality sausage meat or squeeze the filling out of thick pork link sausages—sausages flavored with Italian herbs are good ones to use. If you do use herby sausage meat, it's best to omit the sage in this mixture.

MAKES 12   PREPARATION TIME: 30 MINUTES, PLUS COOLING
COOKING TIME: 20 MINUTES

12 quail eggs
1 teaspoon fennel seeds
1 pound 2 ounces good-quality
   sausage meat
1 tablespoon chopped sage
2 eggs

1⅔ cups fresh bread crumbs
¾ cup plus 2 tablespoons
   all-purpose flour
sunflower oil, for deep-frying
sea salt and freshly ground black pepper

Put the quail eggs in a saucepan, cover with just-boiled water and return to a gentle boil. Cook for 2½ minutes. Drain the eggs and cool them under cold running water, then peel.

Meanwhile, toast the fennel seeds in a dry skillet over medium heat for 1 to 2 minutes until they smell aromatic. Mix together the sausage meat, fennel seeds and sage until combined. Season to taste with salt and pepper.

Beat the eggs in a shallow bowl. Tip the bread crumbs and flour into separate shallow bowls and season the flour to taste with salt and pepper.

Take a heaped tablespoon of the sausage meat in the palm of your hand and flatten it slightly into a circle. Lightly dust a quail egg in the flour, then put it in the middle of the sausage meat. Wrap the sausage meat around the egg, pressing the edges together to seal and make a ball about the size of a golf ball. Dust the Scotch egg in the flour and pat away any excess, then dip it into the egg and roll in the bread crumbs. Put it on a plate and repeat with the remaining ingredients to make 12 Scotch eggs in total.

Heat enough oil in a deep saucepan to deep-fry the Scotch eggs. The oil is hot enough when a small piece of bread turns golden and crisp in 30 seconds. Deep-fry 4 Scotch eggs at a time for 3 to 4 minutes, turning them occasionally until golden brown and crisp all over. Drain them well on paper towels, then leave to one side until completely cool before serving. Repeat to cook the remaining Scotch eggs.

HAM HOCK, ROASTED BEETS & PORCINI LENTILS

This rustic and wholesome dish makes the perfect meal on a cold winter's night when you are looking for something warming and satisfying. It's economical too—a ham hock is still a relatively inexpensive cut of meat. You can, of course, slow-roast the ham hock yourself, but it is far speedier to buy it already cooked. It's delicious with lentils, as here, or with mashed potatoes, cabbage or peas, as well as in soups, stews and roasts.

SERVES 4   PREPARATION TIME: 15 MINUTES   COOKING TIME: 45 MINUTES

3 uncooked beets, peeled and each cut
   into 8 wedges
3 tablespoons olive oil
heaped 1¼ cups green lentils
2 porcini good-quality bouillon cubes
   or 4 chicken bouillon cubes
1 large onion
2 garlic cloves, chopped
1 red bell pepper, halved lengthwise,
   seeded and roughly chopped

8 cherry tomatoes, halved
2 teaspoons dried thyme
2 teaspoons Dijon mustard
juice of 1 lemon
1 handful flat-leaf parsley, roughly
   chopped
1 cup cooked and shredded smoked
   ham hock
sea salt and freshly ground black pepper

Heat the oven to 375°F. Put the beets in a roasting pan and brush 1 tablespoon of the olive oil over. Season to taste with salt and pepper, then bake for 40 to 45 minutes, turning once, until the beets are tender and slightly caramelized.

Meanwhile, put the lentils in a saucepan and pour enough water over to cover them by about ¾ inch. Bring the water to a boil, then crumble in the bouillon cubes and stir until they dissolve. Turn down the heat and simmer, partially covered, for 25 minutes, or until the lentils are tender, then drain.

Heat the remaining oil in a large skillet over medium heat and fry the onion for 8 minutes, or until soft. Add the garlic, red pepper and tomatoes and fry for 3 minutes, or until soft, then stir in the thyme, mustard and lemon juice.

Fold in the parsley, ham hock and lentils, taking care not to break up the lentils, and heat through. Season to taste with pepper before serving with the roasted beets.

COUNTRY-STYLE PÂTÉ

This rustic French pâté is made from economical cuts of pork and flavored with a healthy quantity of garlic, juniper berries, brandy and thyme.

**MAKES ABOUT 2 POUNDS   PREPARATION TIME: 30 MINUTES, PLUS CHILLING
COOKING TIME: 1 HOUR 35 MINUTES**

2 tablespoons butter
1 pound pork liver, trimmed of sinew and
    sliced into strips
12 ounces boneless pork picnic shoulder
    or Boston butt, roughly chopped
12 ounces pork belly, rind cut off and the
    meat roughly chopped
1 tablespoon sea salt

3 garlic cloves, crushed
10 black peppercorns
10 juniper berries
1 teaspoon dried thyme
½ teaspoon ground mace
3 tablespoons brandy
10 to 12 thin slices bacon

Melt the butter in a large skillet and cook the liver in two batches over medium heat for 1½ minutes on each side, or until just colored on the outside.

Grind the liver, picnic shoulder and pork belly in a food processor. Transfer the pork mixture to a bowl. Grind the sea salt with the garlic, peppercorns and juniper berries into a coarse paste, then stir it into the pork mixture with the thyme, mace and brandy. Cover and chill for an hour to let the flavors develop.

Heat the oven to 300°F. Put the bacon between two sheets of plastic wrap and roll out to stretch the slices lengthwise. Set 2 or 3 slices to one side. Line a 2-pint terrine or a 9- x 5-inch bread pan with the rest of the bacon, letting the ends of the slices hang over the rim of the pan.

Spoon the pâté mixture into the terrine and smooth the top, then fold the bacon ends over and lay the reserved slices lengthwise along the top of the pâté to cover it.

Put the terrine in a roasting pan and pour in enough just-boiled water to come halfway up the sides of the terrine. Bake the pâté for 1½ hours, covering it with aluminum foil after 1 hour to prevent it from browning too much, or until the pâté shrinks from the sides of the terrine and the juices run clear when a skewer is inserted into the middle.

Remove the pâté from the roasting pan and leave it to cool completely—the juices surrounding the pâté will gel when cool. The pâté will keep for up to 1 week in the refrigerator.

Smoked Chicken

Smoking is one of the oldest methods of preserving and of adding flavor, and it gives a new dimension to many cuts of meat, poultry and fish. This recipe for hot-smoked chicken doesn't preserve the meat, but it does infuse it with a gentle smokiness while cooking it. You don't need any special equipment: a large wok with a tight-fitting lid does the job perfectly. The smoked chicken makes a great addition to a salad with a creamy dressing and new potatoes. Alternatively, add it to the paella on the facing page.

**SERVES 4   PREPARATION TIME: 15 MINUTES, PLUS MARINATING
COOKING TIME: 18 MINUTES**

heaped 1 teaspoon smoked paprika
2 teaspoons dried oregano
1 tablespoon light brown sugar
½ teaspoon sea salt
4 teaspoons olive oil
4 boneless, skinless chicken breast halves, about 6 ounces each

SMOKING MIXTURE:
4 large handfuls white rice
2 handfuls loose black tea leaves
4 tablespoons Turbinado or Demerara sugar
2 long rosemary sprigs

Mix together the smoked paprika, oregano, brown sugar, salt and olive oil.

Put the chicken between two sheets of plastic wrap and flatten with a meat mallet or rolling pin until about ¾ inch thick. This ensures the chicken cooks evenly and lets the smoke penetrate the meat.

Spread the paprika mixture over the chicken and marinate, covered, in the refrigerator for at least 1 hour.

To prepare the smoker, line the bottom and lid of the wok with foil. Put the wok on a wok stand, if you have one, to keep it stable. Mix together the rice, black tea and Turbinado sugar in the bottom of the wok and lay the rosemary on top. Lightly oil a wire rack and position it above the smoking mixture, making sure it does not touch the mixture.

Put the chicken on the rack and cover with the foil-lined lid. Heat the wok over medium heat until you start to see little wisps of smoke escaping around the lid. Carefully patch up any leaks with foil, turn down the heat to medium-low and make sure the kitchen is well ventilated.

Smoke the chicken for about 18 minutes until it is cooked through: there shouldn't be any trace of pinkness in the juices when the breasts are pierced with a skewer.

PAELLA WITH **SMOKED CHICKEN** & SHRIMP

The smoked chicken adds depth of flavor to this classic Spanish rice dish.

SERVES 4   PREPARATION TIME: 20 MINUTES, PLUS RESTING   COOKING TIME: 45 MINUTES

1 large pinch saffron threads
2 tablespoons olive oil
¾ cup roughly chopped fresh chorizo
1 large onion, finely chopped
1 red bell pepper, seeded and chopped
2 large garlic cloves, chopped
1¾ cups bomba or Calasparra paella rice
¾ cup dry white wine
4¾ cups good-quality hot chicken stock,
　plus extra if needed

1¼ teaspoons hot smoked paprika
¾ recipe quantity Smoked Chicken
　(see facing page), cut into bite-size
　pieces
3 handfuls frozen petit pois or peas
8 raw jumbo shrimp in the shell
12 vine-ripened cherry tomatoes, halved
sea salt and freshly ground black pepper
lemon wedges, to serve

Cover the saffron threads with a little hot water and leave to one side to infuse. Heat the olive oil in a paella dish or large, deep skillet with a lid. Add the chorizo and fry for a few minutes until almost crisp, then, using a slotted spoon, remove it from the pan and leave to one side.

Add the onion to the pan and cook for 5 minutes, or until soft. Add the red pepper and garlic and cook for 2 minutes longer. Add the rice and stir until all the grains are coated and glossy.

Add the wine and when it is bubbling and reduced a little, pour in the stock and the saffron threads with the soaking liquid. Stir in the paprika. Cook over medium-low heat for 15 minutes, without stirring but gently shaking the pan occasionally.

Stir in the chorizo, chicken, peas, shrimp and tomatoes. Season to taste with salt and pepper and continue cooking for 10 to 15 minutes until the rice is tender but still retains its shape and all the ingredients are cooked through; add a little extra stock if the paella looks too dry. Remove the pan from the heat, cover (with a baking sheet if you are using a paella pan) and leave the paella to rest for 5 minutes off the heat. Serve with lemon wedges for squeezing over. Any leftovers can be kept in the refrigerator for up to 2 days.

Bomba Rice

Bomba is considered the king of paella rices. Grown around Valencia, in Spain, this short-grain rice has a soft, yielding texture when cooked, yet keeps its shape. Its name comes from the way each grain expands widthwise during cooking to form "little bombs." One of the key features of this ancient strain of rice is its absorbency, so it takes on all the flavors of the stock and other ingredients in the paella.

Confit of Duck

Confiting is an ancient way of preserving foods, such as meat, poultry, fish or vegetables, for the long winter months when there wasn't much fresh food available. It is still very popular in French cuisine. Confit of Duck makes a delicious foundation for many meals, including the traditional Cassoulet (see facing page). You can also scrape the fat from the duck legs and roast them in a hot oven (400°F) for 15 minutes, or until the skin crisps. Serve with a green salad, or mashed potatoes and red cabbage, or with Puy lentils.

**SERVES 4   PREPARATION TIME: 10 MINUTES, PLUS OVERNIGHT SALTING
AND 1 WEEK MATURING   COOKING TIME: 1 HOUR 40 MINUTES**

4 good-size fatty duck legs
4 teaspoons coarse sea salt
1 tablespoon black peppercorns
3 garlic cloves, sliced
2 bay leaves, torn into pieces
4 thyme sprigs

FOR CONFITING:
about 4 cups duck or goose fat
2 bay leaves
6 garlic cloves, peeled
a few thyme sprigs

Put the duck legs in a nonmetallic dish and sprinkle the salt, peppercorns, garlic, bay leaves and thyme over the flesh side of each leg. Cover the dish with plastic wrap and leave in the refrigerator overnight.

Heat the oven to 300°F. Brush the salt, pepper and other flavorings off the duck, then rinse the legs under cold running water and pat dry with paper towels.

Cut away any loose bits of skin and put these in a large Dutch oven, along with the duck legs, skin-side down; ideally you want them to be in a single layer. Cook the duck legs over low heat until the fat starts to run, then turn up the heat and cook for a few minutes longer to color the skin.

Turn the duck over and pour in the duck or goose fat to cover. Add the bay leaves, garlic and thyme and heat until the fat melts. Cover the pot with a lid and transfer it to the oven for 1½ hours, or until the duck legs are very tender.

Leave the duck legs to cool slightly in the pot, then transfer them to a sterilized crock or large canning jar. Pour the fat over the legs so they are completely submerged, leaving any duck juices behind in the bottom of the Dutch oven. Leave the confit to cool completely, then cover and store in the refrigerator for 1 week before eating, to let the flavors mature. Store for up to 3 months in the refrigerator.

CASSOULET WITH **CONFIT OF DUCK**

This classic French slow-cooked stew typically contains a hearty mixture of white beans, confit of duck, bacon and sausages. Rich, warming and filling, it makes a great winter dish.

**SERVES 4   PREPARATION TIME: 20 MINUTES, PLUS OVERNIGHT SOAKING
COOKING TIME: 2¾ HOURS**

1 cup dried white beans, such as
  cannellini, great northern or navy
½ recipe quantity Confit of Duck
  (see facing page)
6 ounces thick-cut bacon, cut into
  ¼-inch lardons
12 ounces boneless pork picnic shoulder
  or Boston butt, cut into large bite-size
  pieces and trimmed of fat
1 large onion, chopped
2 carrots, chopped
1 celery stick, sliced
2 bay leaves

2 teaspoons dried thyme
1 cup hard cider or dry white wine
heaped 1 cup chopped tomatoes
2 good-quality chicken bouillon cubes
heaped 1 cup sliced smoked sausage
freshly ground black pepper
steamed kale and French bread, to serve

TOPPING:
1 tablespoon olive oil
2 cups fresh bread crumbs
1 large garlic clove, crushed
2 tablespoons chopped parsley leaves

Put the beans in a large bowl and pour enough cold water over to cover. Leave to soak, covered, overnight. The next day, drain the beans and rinse under cold running water. Put them in a large saucepan and cover with plenty of fresh water. Bring to a boil, then leave to bubble away for 15 minutes. Drain the beans and leave them to one side.

Meanwhile, heat a large Dutch oven. Scrape off the fat surrounding the duck and sear the meat in the hot pot, skin-side down, for a few minutes until brown and crisp. Remove the duck and drain on paper towels.

Pour off all but 1 tablespoon of the fat from the Dutch oven and add the bacon. Fry, stirring occasionally, for 5 minutes, or until starting to become crisp. Leave to drain on paper towels. Repeat with the pieces of pork.

Heat the oven to 315°F. Add the onion, carrots and celery to the Dutch oven and cook for 5 minutes, or until soft. Return the bacon, duck and pork to the pot and add the half-cooked white beans, bay leaves, thyme, cider, 2¼ cups water and the tomatoes. Bring to a boil, then turn down the heat and stir in the bouillon cubes and smoked sausage. Cover the pot with the lid and transfer it to the oven to cook for 1 hour. Remove the lid and cook for 1 hour longer, or until the sauce reduces and thickens and the beans are tender. Season to taste with pepper (you are unlikely to need salt).

Meanwhile, make the topping. Heat the oil in a skillet over medium heat and fry the bread crumbs for 4 minutes, or until starting to color. Add the garlic and cook for 2 to 3 minutes longer until the crumbs are crisp and golden. Remove the skillet from the heat and stir in the parsley. Sprinkle the topping over the cassoulet and serve with kale and French bread.

MERGUEZ SAUSAGES & SMOKED PAPRIKA BEANS

Originating in North Africa, these thin, dark sausages are made from lamb or mutton (sometimes beef) and are heavily spiced, often with harissa. This dish makes a simple weekday meal. Look for butter bean gigantes in Middle Eastern or Spanish food stores; if you can't find any, use ordinary canned butter beans or lima beans instead.

SERVES 4   PREPARATION TIME: 15 MINUTES   COOKING TIME: 17 MINUTES

10 merguez sausages
3 tablespoons olive oil, plus extra
    for brushing
1 red bell pepper, seeded and
    roughly chopped
4 cloves garlic, finely chopped
3 large vine-ripened tomatoes, quartered,
    seeded and chopped
1 tablespoon thyme leaves
1 teaspoon hot smoked paprika

2 jars (15-oz.) butter bean gigantes or 2 cans
    (15-oz.) butter beans or lima beans,
    drained and rinsed
3 handfuls baby spinach leaves
1 teaspoon Dijon mustard
juice of 1 lemon
4 large, thick slices country-style bread
sea salt and freshly ground black pepper
small handful cilantro leaves,
    for sprinkling

Heat the broiler to high. Broil the sausages, turning them occasionally, for 10 to 12 minutes, depending on their thickness, until cooked through. Thickly slice the sausages and set to one side.

Meanwhile, heat half the olive oil in a large skillet and fry the red pepper for 3 minutes, or until soft. Add the garlic and cook for 1 minute longer. Add the tomatoes, thyme, paprika and butter beans and cook, stirring regularly, for about 10 minutes.

Add the spinach and a splash of water and cook until the leaves wilt, then stir in the mustard, lemon juice and the sausages. Season to taste with salt and pepper and heat through.

Heat a large cast-iron, ridged grill pan. Brush the slices of bread with the remaining olive oil and grill for 5 minutes, turning once, until slightly charred in places. (You might need to do this in two batches.)

Serve the sausages and beans spooned on top of the grilled bread with the cilantro leaves sprinkled over.

SAUSAGES WITH APPLE & ONION-SEED CHUTNEY

Choose thick, herby link sausages with a high meat content for this comforting, one-pan dish. The sausages are immersed in a lightly spiced apple chutney so they take on its flavor, and are great served with mashed potatoes and green vegetables.

SERVES 4   PREPARATION TIME: 15 MINUTES   COOKING TIME: 35 MINUTES

8 fat, herb-flavored link sausages
2 tablespoons olive oil
1 large onion, chopped
1 teaspoon onion seeds
3 apples, peeled, cored and diced
1 tablespoon apple cider vinegar

1 tablespoon thyme leaves, plus extra
    for sprinkling
1 to 2 teaspoons light brown sugar
1 to 2 teaspoons Dijon mustard
sea salt and freshly ground black pepper

Heat the broiler. Broil the sausages for 15 to 18 minutes until brown all over.

Meanwhile, heat the olive oil in a large, deep skillet over medium heat and cook the onion for 10 minutes, or until soft. Add the onion seeds and cook 1 minute longer, or until they smell slightly toasted.

Add the apples, vinegar and ½ cup water. Stir, then cover and simmer for 15 minutes over medium-low heat, until the apples are soft.

Crush the apples with the back of a fork to break them down slightly, then add the thyme, and sugar and mustard to taste, stirring to dissolve the sugar. Season to taste with salt and pepper.

Transfer the sausages to the pan and heat them in the chutney for 4 to 5 minutes until warmed through. Add a splash of water if the chutney looks too dry. Serve the sausages with the apple chutney, sprinkled with a few thyme leaves.

Choosing Sausages

Pork and apple are natural partners, with the sweet acidity of the fruit cutting through the rich fattiness of the meat. Having said that, you can experiment with different types of sausages: try venison or lamb, or a vegetarian alternative. Or perhaps blood pudding? Sausages with flavorings such as thyme, parsley, fennel seeds and garlic work well with the fruit chutney. Bear in mind that sausages need a certain amount of fat, and bread crumbs give them a lighter texture, so choose sausages made with 80 to 90 percent meat.

SLOW-COOKED MEXICAN PULLED PORK WITH PICKLED RED CABBAGE

Here, pork is braised so slowly in a barbecue sauce it almost falls apart. Serve it shredded with pickled red cabbage, which, if made in advance, becomes iridescent in color.

**SERVES 4   PREPARATION TIME: 25 MINUTES, PLUS RESTING
COOKING TIME: 2 HOURS 20 MINUTES**

2¾ pounds boneless pork Boston butt, any skin removed
1 tablespoon sunflower oil
1 teaspoon hot smoked paprika
1 teaspoon English mustard powder
½ teaspoon ground ginger
4 tablespoons ketchup
2 tablespoons apple cider vinegar
2 teaspoons Worcestershire sauce
½ teaspoon salt
2 tablespoons dark brown sugar
1 large onion, cut into 8 wedges
juice of 1 large orange
1 handful oregano sprigs

PICKLED RED CABBAGE:
1½ cups shredded red cabbage
1 large carrot, coarsely grated
2 teaspoons sugar
juice of 1 lime
2 tablespoons apple cider vinegar
sea salt and freshly ground black pepper

TO SERVE:
8 to 12 taco shells
shredded hearts of lettuce
4 tablespoons sour cream
1 small handful cilantro leaves

Heat the oven to 300°F. Cut off as much fat as you can from the pork. Heat the oil in a large Dutch oven over medium heat and sear the pork until browned all over. Transfer the pork to a plate.

Mix together the hot smoked paprika, mustard powder, ginger, ketchup, vinegar, Worcestershire sauce, salt and brown sugar. Spread two-thirds of the mixture all over the pork. Put the onion in an even layer in the pot and top it with the pork. Pour in the orange juice with 2 tablespoons water. Scatter the oregano over the top. Cover the pot and place in the oven to cook for 2 hours, occasionally spooning the juices over the pork.

Meanwhile, to make the pickle, put the cabbage and carrot in a nonmetallic serving bowl. Stir the sugar, lime juice and vinegar together until the sugar dissolves. Season to taste with salt and pepper, then pour over the vegetables and stir. Leave to one side.

After the pork has cooked for 2 hours, remove and discard the onions, then transfer the pork to a plate, cover with foil and leave to rest for 15 minutes. Increase the oven temperature to 350°F.

Put the Dutch oven with the reserved sauce on the stovetop and pour in any juices from the resting meat. Bring to a boil, then turn down the heat and simmer until the liquid reduces and thickens. At the same time warm the taco shells in the oven for a few minutes. Using two forks, shred the pork and discard any fat. Put the pork on a large serving plate, pour the sauce over and stir the meat until coated. Fill each taco shell with a little lettuce and top with the pork, pickled cabbage, a spoonful of sour cream and cilantro leaves.

BAKED CURRANT- & CLOVE-GLAZED HAM

There is something magnificent about a baked ham, with its glazed golden-brown crust and succulent meat. Ham, from the hind leg of the hog, is most commonly cured, much the same way as bacon, as well as smoked, and is sold fully cooked, partially cooked or uncooked. This recipe starts with cooking the meat, but you can buy a fully-cooked ham and skip the roasting process. The ham is equally good served warm or cold and thinly sliced.

**SERVES 4 TO 6   PREPARATION TIME: 20 MINUTES, PLUS RESTING
   COOKING TIME: 1 HOUR 55 MINUTES**

1 boneless ham, about 3 pounds 5 ounces
15 juniper berries, lightly crushed with
   the flat of a knife blade
2 bay leaves
3 tablespoons red currant jelly

heaped 1 teaspoon Dijon mustard
finely grated zest of 1 orange and juice
   of ½ orange
10–20 cloves, to taste

Put the ham in a large saucepan with cold water to cover, cover the pan and bring slowly to a boil, then drain and discard the water.

Return the ham to the pan, cover with fresh cold water and add the juniper berries and bay leaves. Return to a boil, then turn down the heat and simmer, partially covered, for 1 hour, or until cooked through. (Allow 20 minutes per 18 ounces.) Drain the ham, discarding the juniper berries and bay leaves.

Twenty minutes before the end of the calculated cooking time, heat the oven to 400°F. Put the red currant jelly, mustard and orange zest and juice in a small saucepan over medium heat. Stir until the jelly melts, then simmer for 10 to 15 minutes until the mixture reduces and thickens to a syrupy consistency.

Leave the ham to cool slightly, then remove and discard the skin, leaving an outer layer of fat. Pat the fat dry with paper towels. Using a sharp knife, score the fat diagonally, then change direction and score the fat in the opposite direction to form a diamond pattern. Push the cloves into the fat, making sure they are fairly evenly spaced, then spoon the red-currant glaze over the top.

Put the ham into a roasting pan and bake, basting occasionally, for 25 to 30 minutes, until the top is golden brown and caramelized. Remove the ham from the oven, cover loosely with foil and leave to rest for about 15 minutes before carving and serving.

STEAK & ALE POTPIES

These individual beef and vegetable potpies are topped with a of hot-water pastry crust, which has a rich, golden exterior and crisp texture. This piecrust differs from other versions of hot-water pastry in that it contains egg and butter, instead of the usual lard, so it has a softer texture, and, more interestingly, you leave it to cool before rolling it out. The trick is to roll out the dough between sheets of plastic wrap, which helps it to hold together and makes it more manageable. If time is against you, however, use bought puff pastry dough. Serve with mashed potatoes, celery root or rutabaga—or a combination—to soak up the delicious rich gravy.

MAKES 4   PREPARATION TIME: 30 MINUTES, PLUS CHILLING   COOKING TIME: 2¼ HOURS

FILLING:
3 to 4 tablespoons olive oil
1¾ pounds boneless braising beef,
    cut into bite-size pieces, fat trimmed
2 tablespoons all-purpose flour
4 carrots, roughly chopped
3 cups baby button mushrooms
2 onions, sliced
3 garlic cloves, chopped
1¼ cups ale
2 cups plus 2 tablespoons good-quality
    beef stock

2 teaspoons dried thyme
2 bay leaves
sea salt and freshly ground black pepper

PASTRY DOUGH:
1¾ cups plus 2 tablespoons all-purpose
    flour
a pinch salt
1 egg
5 tablespoons butter
1 egg, beaten, for glazing

To make the filling, heat 1 tablespoon of the olive oil in a Dutch oven over medium heat. Dust the beef with seasoned flour, then sear in batches until browned all over. Add a little extra oil when necessary. Using a slotted spoon, remove the beef and leave to one side.

Add another tablespoon of the oil to the pot and fry the carrots and mushrooms for 5 minutes, or until soft and brown. Remove the vegetables from the pot and leave to one side.

Add the remaining oil to the pot, if needed, and fry the onions for 5 minutes, then add the garlic and fry for 1 minute longer, or until soft and golden brown.

Return the beef, carrots and mushrooms to the pot and pour in the ale. Bring to a boil and boil until the ale reduces by half. Add the stock, thyme and bay leaves and stir to combine. Return to a boil, then turn down the heat and simmer, covered, for 1 hour. Uncover, stir and continue simmering the stew for 30 minutes, or until the beef is tender and the gravy is reduced and thickened. Season to taste with salt and pepper.

While the beef is cooking, make the dough. Sift the flour and salt into a mixing bowl. Make a well in the middle and add the egg. Put the butter and 7 tablespoons water in a pan and heat gently, stirring occasionally, until the butter melts, then bring the mixture to a boil.

Pour the butter mixture into the bowl containing the flour and mix with a wooden spoon to form a sticky

CONTINUED ON PAGE **42**

dough. Tip the dough onto a large plate and spread out, using the back of the wooden spoon. Leave to cool for about 10 minutes or until cool enough to handle. Knead the dough into a ball (it's similar to a sticky paste and should hold together), then wrap it in plastic wrap and chill for 30 minutes to firm up.

Heat the oven to 425°F. Divide the beef filling among four 4-inch-deep pie dishes, or other similar baking dishes with rims, and put on a large cookie sheet.

Divide the dough into 5 equal pieces. Roll out 4 pieces individually between sheets of plastic wrap into ovals or rounds to make the pie lids, each about ½ inch larger than the top of a dish. Roll out the remaining piece of dough and cut it into 4 strips the same width as the rim of the pie dishes and long enough to fit all the way around the top of a dish.

Brush the rim of each dish with a little beaten egg. Lay a dough strip around the rim of a dish and brush with more egg. Drape a dough lid over the top and press the edges together to seal. Trim off any excess dough, then crimp the edge. Repeat to cover all the pies, then brush the lids with the remaining egg. Prick the lids a few times with a fork and decorate with any dough trimmings, if you like.

Bake for 10 minutes, then reduce the oven temperature to 400°F and bake for 20 to 25 minutes longer until the pastry is golden and cooked through.

Braising Beef

These pies require a cut of beef that becomes succulent and tender when slowly cooked over low heat. Perfect for this are the parts of the cow that do the most work, such as the legs, chuck (from the shoulder), shank or bottom round. Also called stewing meat, these cuts can be tough if not cooked very slowly to become tender, but they are usually very tasty. When buying braising beef, look for a good marbling of fat running through the meat; it will break down during cooking and add lots of flavor.

Cuts from parts of the cow that get little exercise, such as the tenderloin or sirloin, however, have the best texture and flavor when cooked quickly (pan-fried, broiled or roasted) with high heat.

VENISON WELLINGTON

Perfect for a special dinner party, this venison tenderloin wrapped in puff pastry has layers of prosciutto slices, mushroom duxelles and chicken liver parfait. If you can't find venison, a beef tenderloin can be used instead. The mushroom duxelles, which is similar to a coarse pâté, can also be served as an appetizer spread on thin slices of toast.

**SERVES 6 TO 8   PREPARATION TIME: 25 MINUTES, PLUS SOAKING, COOLING AND RESTING
COOKING TIME: 1 HOUR 5 MINUTES**

olive oil, for brushing
1 venison tenderloin, about 2 pounds, trimmed of any fat
13 ounces puff pastry dough
all-purpose flour, for dusting
1 medium egg, beaten
3½ ounces thinly sliced prosciutto
¾ cup chicken liver parfait or pâté
sea salt and freshly ground black pepper

MUSHROOM DUXELLES:
¾ ounce dried porcini mushrooms
3 tablespoons butter
5¾ cups finely chopped portobello mushrooms
4 thyme sprigs, leaves removed
5 tablespoons fresh white bread crumbs

Cover the porcini mushrooms with just-boiled water and leave for 20 minutes, or until soft. Meanwhile, brush olive oil all over the venison and season to taste with salt and pepper. Heat a large, deep skillet over high heat and sear the venison until browned all over. Put it on a wire rack over a plate and leave to cool.

To make the duxelles, drain the porcini, reserving the soaking liquid, and squeeze out any excess water, then finely chop. Melt the butter in the skillet over medium heat. Add the porcini and portobello mushrooms and cook, stirring, for 20 minutes, or until they are soft and there isn't any trace of liquid. Season and stir in the thyme and bread crumbs. Transfer to a shallow bowl and leave to cool.

Heat the oven to 400°F and line a baking sheet with parchment paper. Cut off one-third of the dough and roll it out on a lightly floured countertop until about 2 inches wider and longer than the venison. Put the dough on the lined baking sheet and brush it with beaten egg.

Arrange the prosciutto on top of the dough to make a layer about the same size as the venison. Set the venison on the prosciutto and spread the chicken liver parfait evenly over the meat. Spoon the mushroom duxelles over the top, pressing it so it sticks to the parfait.

Roll out the remaining dough on the lightly floured countertop until large enough to cover the venison. Brush the dough surrounding the venison with beaten egg, then drape the rolled-out dough over the top. Press the dough edges together around the venison to seal, then trim off any excess. Crimp the edges with a fork and prick the top in several places. Decorate with the dough trimmings.

Brush the Wellington with the remaining beaten egg. Bake for 20 minutes, then reduce the oven temperature to 350°F and bake for 10 minutes longer, or until the pastry is golden brown and cooked through. Remove the Wellington from the oven and leave to stand for 10 minutes before slicing.

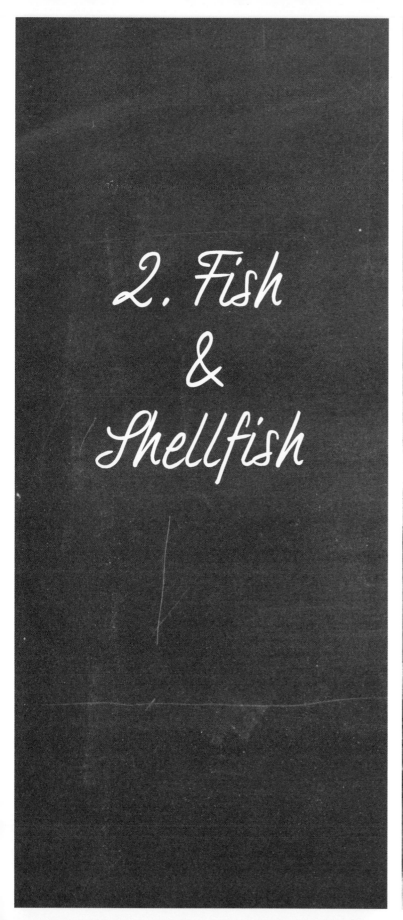

2. Fish & Shellfish

Fresh Marinated Anchovies

Marinated pickled anchovies are a familiar sight in deli chill cabinets. Here, the small, slender fish are preserved in vinegar and flavored with garlic, red onion and parsley until lightly cured.

SERVES 4 TO 6   PREPARATION TIME: 1 HOUR, PLUS 2 DAYS MARINATING

10 ounces fresh anchovies or small sardines, rinsed and patted dry
1 tablespoon sea salt
6 tablespoons white wine vinegar
2 garlic cloves, thinly sliced
2 tablespoons lemon juice
2 tablespoons extra virgin olive oil
½ small red onion, finely chopped
2 tablespoons chopped flat-leaf parsley

Cut each anchovy down the belly and open up. To remove the backbone, run your finger down it, separating the flesh from the bone and gently prising it out. Remove the head and tail and lift out the backbone. You will be left with whole, butterflied anchovies.

Put the anchovies, flesh-side up, in a single layer in a nonmetallic dish and sprinkle lightly with the salt. Mix the vinegar with 1 tablespoon water and spoon the mixture over the anchovies. Scatter the garlic over, cover the dish with plastic wrap and refrigerate for 48 hours. The fish will turn white.

Drain the anchovies and discard the liquid. Rinse them briefly under cold running water, pat dry and put them in a clean dish. Spoon the lemon juice and olive oil over them and sprinkle with the red onion and parsley. The fish are ready to eat now, but will keep for up to 1 week in the refrigerator.

PISSALADIÈRE WITH **MARINATED ANCHOVIES**

This Provençal classic is topped with a generous amount of slowly cooked onions, as well as anchovies, olives and thyme. Marinated fresh anchovies are a twist on the traditional thin, brown, salted ones or those packed in oil.

SERVES 6   PREPARATION TIME: 20 MINUTES, PLUS RISING   COOKING TIME: 1¼ HOURS

2 cups all-purpose flour, plus extra
   for dusting
1 teaspoon salt
1½ teaspoons instant active dry yeast
½ teaspoon sugar
1 egg, lightly beaten
3 tablespoons olive oil, plus extra
   for greasing

2¼ pounds white onions, thinly sliced
2 large cloves garlic, crushed
1 tablespoon thyme leaves
6 Fresh Marinated Anchovies (see facing
   page), halved lengthwise into thin strips
1 handful black olives
freshly ground black pepper

To make the dough, mix together the flour, salt, yeast and sugar in a large bowl. Add the egg, 1 tablespoon of the oil and 5 tablespoons warm water (120° to 130°F). Mix until the dough comes together, adding a little more water if it is too dry. Turn the dough onto a lightly floured countertop and knead for 5 minutes, or until it forms a smooth ball. Put the dough in a greased bowl, cover and leave to rise while you cook the onions.

Heat the remaining olive oil in a large, nonstick skillet over medium heat. Add the onions, turn down the heat to low, cover and cook, stirring occasionally, for 30 minutes, or until the onions are meltingly soft, but not colored. Uncover 10 minutes before the end of the cooking time to reduce any liquid in the pan. Add the garlic and cook for 1 minute longer. Remove the pan from the heat and leave the onions to cool slightly.

Meanwhile, heat the oven to 425°F. Lightly oil a 15- x 10-inch baking sheet or jelly roll pan. Roll out the dough and use to line the baking sheet, pressing the dough up the sides.

Spoon the onion mixture on top of the dough, then sprinkle with the thyme and arrange the anchovies on top in a crisscross pattern. Season to taste with pepper and top with the olives. Bake for 25 to 30 minutes until the crust is baked through and golden brown. Serve warm, cut into wedges.

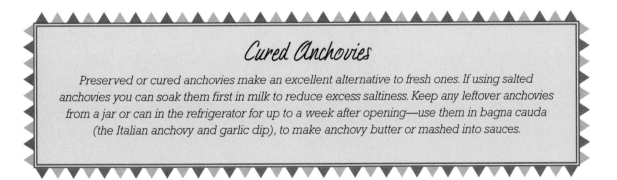

Cured Anchovies

Preserved or cured anchovies make an excellent alternative to fresh ones. If using salted anchovies you can soak them first in milk to reduce excess saltiness. Keep any leftover anchovies from a jar or can in the refrigerator for up to a week after opening—use them in bagna cauda (the Italian anchovy and garlic dip), to make anchovy butter or mashed into sauces.

Crab Terrine

Crabmeat gives this simple terrine a delicious flavor and texture. Light as a feather, the creamy terrine makes a perfect topping for thin, crisp Melba toast, crostini or crackers. Alternatively, serve it with a green salad and crusty bread for a more substantial lunch.

SERVES 8 TO 10   PREPARATION TIME: 25 MINUTES, PLUS CHILLING
COOKING TIME: 5 MINUTES

1 cup plus 2 tablespoons good-quality fish stock
2 envelopes (¼-oz.) unflavored gelatin
1 pound crabmeat
2 tablespoons lemon juice
a good dash hot-pepper sauce
½ teaspoon sea salt
1 cup plus 2 tablespoons crème fraîche or sour cream
1 extra-large egg white
ground white pepper
paprika, for dusting

MELBA TOAST:
slices of day-old wholewheat or white bread

Heat the stock in a small saucepan and stir in the gelatin until the granules dissolve. Remove the pan from the heat and leave the gelatin to cool slightly just until it begins to set.

Put the crabmeat in a large mixing bowl. Fold in the dissolved gelatin, lemon juice, hot-pepper sauce, salt and crème fraîche until combined, taking care not to break up the crabmeat too much.

Beat the egg white in a clean, greasefree bowl until it forms stiff peaks. Using a metal spoon, fold it into the crabmeat mixture. Season to taste with white pepper. Pour the mixture into a 2-pint terrine or baking dish, cover with plastic wrap and put in the refrigerator to set. It will take a few hours to become firm and set to a light, mousselike texture. Before serving, turn the terrine out onto a serving plate and dust the top with paprika. The terrine will keep for up to 3 days in the refrigerator.

To make the Melba toast, heat the broiler and toast the bread until golden on both sides. Cut off the crusts, then carefully cut each slice of toast horizontally into 2 thin pieces and cut each piece diagonally into 2 triangles. Toast the untoasted side of each triangular piece of bread until golden and crisp. Leave to cool before serving with the terrine.

CREAMY **CRAB TERRINE** & SCALLION TART

If you have any leftover Crab Terrine, use it as the base of this seafood tart, flavored with thin slices of scallion and flecks of red chili. You don't want the chilies to be too pronounced, but just hot enough to cut through the richness of the crab and add a slight kick.

SERVES 6 PREPARATION TIME: 30 MINUTES, PLUS CHILLING COOKING TIME: 55 MINUTES

PASTRY DOUGH:
1⅔ cups all-purpose flour, plus extra
   for dusting
a large pinch salt
6 tablespoons cold butter, diced, plus
   extra for greasing
1 egg yolk, beaten

FILLING:
1 tablespoon olive oil
3 scallions, finely chopped
2 red chilies, seeded and finely chopped
¼ recipe quantity Crab Terrine
   (see facing page)
4 extra-large eggs, lightly beaten
¾ cup plus 2 tablespoons whole milk
5 ounces crabmeat
sea salt and freshly ground black pepper

First make the dough. Sift the flour and salt into a mixing bowl and cut in the butter until it resembles coarse bread crumbs. Using a table knife, stir in the egg yolk and enough water, about 2 tablespoons, to bring the dough together. Alternatively, you can use a food processor to make the dough.

Tip out the dough onto a lightly floured countertop and form into a smooth ball. Wrap in plastic wrap, flatten slightly into a disk and chill for 30 minutes.

Heat the oven to 375°F and lightly grease a 10-inch fluted tart pan with a removable bottom with butter.

Roll out the dough on the lightly floured surface and use to line the prepared tart pan. Leave the excess dough hanging over the top of the pan. Prick the bottom of the pastry shell with a fork, then line with parchment paper and fill with baking beans. Bake for 15 minutes. Remove the baking beans and paper and bake for 10 minutes longer, or until the pastry is cooked and light golden. Remove the pastry shell from the oven and trim the edge. Reduce the oven temperature to 325°F.

While the tart shell is baking, make the filling. Heat the olive oil and fry the scallions and chilies for 2 to 3 minutes over medium heat until soft. Remove the pan from the heat and leave the scallions and chillies to cool.

In a large bowl, mix the crab terrine into the eggs and milk until combined. Stir in the crabmeat, scallions and chilies. Season to taste with salt and pepper. Pour the mixture into the pastry shell. Bake for 30 minutes, or until the filling is just firm. Leave to cool slightly on a wire rack before serving.

WARM SQUID & CHORIZO SALAD

To prepare succulent squid you need either to cook it over low heat for a long time or quickly over fairly high heat. In this recipe, the squid should be cooked very briefly—just a minute or so in a hot grill pan will guarantee it is wonderfully tender. Any leftover garlic and herb oil will keep in the refrigerator for up to 1 week.

SERVES 4   PREPARATION TIME: 25 MINUTES   COOKING TIME: 20 MINUTES

1 pound 7 ounces squid
extra virgin olive oil, for frying
heaped 1 cup thickly sliced chorizo,
    casing removed
3 ounces arugula leaves
crusty bread, to serve

GARLIC & HERB OIL:
½ cup extra virgin olive oil
juice of ½ lemon
2 garlic cloves, preferably new season,
    crushed
1 red chili, seeded and finely chopped
1 handful flat-leaf parsley, finely chopped
3 basil sprigs, leaves torn into
    small pieces
sea salt and freshly ground black pepper

To make the garlic and herb oil, pour the olive oil into a small bowl and beat in the lemon juice. Next, stir in the garlic, chili, parsley and basil, then season to taste with salt and pepper. Leave to one side until ready to serve.

To prepare the squid, remove the intestines by pulling the tentacles and insides away from the body. Cut the tentacles just below the eyes and leave to one side. Discard the eyes and intestines. Pull out the plasticlike quill from the body cavity and discard. Rinse out the body to remove any remaining entrails. Peel off any exterior brown-pink membrane, then rinse the squid again.

Cut the squid into 2-inch pieces and lightly score the inside of each piece with the tip of a small, sharp knife. Cover and refrigerate the squid and tentacles until needed.

Heat a splash of olive oil in a skillet over medium heat and cook the chorizo for about 3 minutes, turning once, until almost crisp. Remove from the pan and drain on paper towels. Cut into small bite-size pieces and leave to one side.

Heat a large cast-iron, ridged grill pan over high heat until very hot. Brush the pieces of squid with a little oil and grill them for about 30 seconds on each side, pressing the squid onto the hot ridges of the pan, until opaque and marked by the ridges. You will need to do this in batches.

Make a bed of arugula on a serving plate. Lay the squid and chorizo on the arugula, spoon the garlic and herb oil over the top and serve immediately with crusty bread.

HOT MACKEREL NIÇOISE

This is a twist on the classic Provençal salad, using flakes of hot smoked mackerel instead of the usual canned tuna.

SERVES 4   PREPARATION TIME: 30 MINUTES   COOKING TIME: 20 MINUTES

18 ounces new potatoes, scrubbed
and halved if large
2 extra-large eggs
5 large vine-ripened tomatoes
4 ounces thin green beans, trimmed
about 3 cups watercress
1 heart of lettuce, leaves separated and
large leaves sliced
½ English cucumber, quartered
lengthwise, seeded and cut into chunks
1 small red onion, cut into thin rings
⅓ cup black olives, such as Kalamata
olives

1 small handful flat-leaf parsley, leaves
roughly chopped
12 ounces smoked mackerel fillets

DRESSING:
½ teaspoon sea salt flakes
1 garlic clove, peeled
1 teaspoon English mustard powder
1 tablespoon white wine vinegar
7 tablespoons extra virgin olive oil
2 tablespoons snipped chives
freshly ground black pepper

Cook the potatoes in a pan of boiling salted water for 15 minutes, or until tender. Drain and leave to one side. Meanwhile, boil the eggs for 8 minutes, after which time the whites should be set and the yolks still slightly runny. Drain and cool slightly under cold running water, then peel and cut into quarters.

Using a small, sharp knife, cut a shallow cross in the bottom of each tomato, then put them in a heatproof bowl and cover with just-boiled water. Leave to stand for 2 minutes, then drain. Peel off and discard the tomato skins, then seed and cut the flesh into large chunks. Leave to one side.

Steam the green beans for 5 minutes, or until just tender, then refresh briefly under cold running water; you want them to be slightly warm and crisp.

To make the dressing, pound the salt flakes and garlic to a paste using a mortar and pestle. Stir in the mustard powder, then add the vinegar and stir until the salt dissolves. Pour in the olive oil and beat with a fork until combined. Stir in the chives, season with pepper and leave to one side.

Put the watercress and lettuce in a large serving bowl and scatter the potatoes, tomatoes, cucumber, red onion, olives and parsley over. Top with the green beans. Pour half of the dressing over and toss the salad until combined.

Heat a large skillet over medium heat and warm through the mackerel for 3 minutes, turning once, until slightly crisp on the surface. Remove the mackerel from the heat and peel off the skin. Break the mackerel fillets into large flakes and put on top of the salad with the eggs, then drizzle more of the dressing over to taste. Serve while the mackerel is still warm.

SMOKED FISH & CLAM CHOWDER

Evaporated milk is the surprise ingredient in this chowder, adding a rich creaminess to the sauce. You can serve the chowder, as is the custom in San Francisco, in large, hollowed-out sourdough rolls.

SERVES 4   PREPARATION TIME: 15 MINUTES   COOKING TIME: 25 MINUTES

1 pound 5 ounces undyed smoked
   haddock fillets (finnan haddie)
1¾ cups milk
1 tablespoon sunflower oil
2 slices smoked bacon, finely chopped
2 onions, finely chopped
1 bay leaf
2 carrots, diced

2 cups peeled and diced potatoes
3½ cups good-quality fish stock or
   vegetable stock
4 tablespoons evaporated milk
10 ounces bottled clams, drained and well
   rinsed, especially if they are in vinegar
freshly ground black pepper
snipped chives, for sprinkling

Put the smoked haddock flesh-side down in a large, deep skillet and pour the milk over the top. Bring to a boil, then turn down the heat to low and simmer for 8 minutes, or until the fish is just cooked through and flakes easily. Remove the haddock with a spatula, transfer to a plate and leave to one side. Strain the milk, discarding the solids, and leave to one side.

Meanwhile, heat the sunflower oil in a large saucepan and fry the bacon for 2 minutes, or until beginning to brown. Add the onions and cook for 5 minutes longer, or until the onion is soft. Stir in the bay leaf, carrots and potatoes and cook for 5 minutes longer.

Pour the stock into the pan and bring to a boil, then turn down the heat to low and simmer, partially covered, for 10 minutes, or until the carrots and potatoes are tender.

While the vegetables are cooking, remove and discard the skin and bones from the haddock fillets, then flake the flesh into large chunks. Add the reserved milk, evaporated milk, cooked haddock and clams to the saucepan. Season to taste with pepper (you are unlikely to need salt because the fish is very salty) and heat for a few minutes. Serve sprinkled with chives.

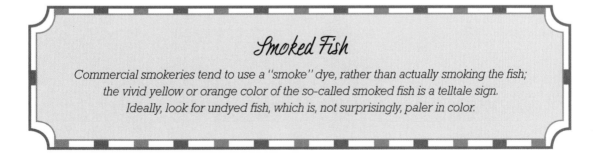

Smoked Fish

Commercial smokeries tend to use a "smoke" dye, rather than actually smoking the fish; the vivid yellow or orange color of the so-called smoked fish is a telltale sign. Ideally, look for undyed fish, which is, not surprisingly, paler in color.

Salmon Gravlax with Lemon & Ginger

Make sure you buy the freshest salmon for gravlax. Ideally you should use a piece cut from the middle of the fillet, which won't be as thin as the tail end and not too thick to take on the flavors of the marinade. Finely grated lemon zest and fresh gingerroot make a flavorful alternative to the more traditional dill.

SERVES 4 AS A LIGHT MEAL OR 6 AS AN APPETIZER
PREPARATION TIME: 15 MINUTES, PLUS 2 DAYS MARINATING

18 ounces middle-cut salmon fillet
6 tablespoons coarse sea salt
scant ½ cup sugar
finely grated zest of 2 lemons
1-inch piece fresh gingerroot, peeled and grated
1 tablespoon lemon juice
freshly ground black pepper (optional)

Using a pair of tweezers, remove any bones from the salmon. Lay the salmon, flesh-side down, in a nonmetallic dish. Mix the salt and sugar together and sprinkle half the mixture over the skin in an even layer, then turn the salmon over and sprinkle with the remaining salt and sugar mixture, making sure the fish is completely covered. Cover the dish with plastic wrap. Put a plate on top of the salmon and weight it down to encourage the curing process. Leave in the refrigerator for 24 hours, turning after 12 hours.

Remove the salmon from the refrigerator and wipe away all the salt and sugar. Gently rinse under running cold water, then pat dry and return the salmon, flesh-side up, to the dry, clean dish.

Mix the lemon zest and gingerroot together and scatter them over the salmon until it is covered, pressing the flavorings into the flesh, then sprinkle sparingly with the lemon juice. Season to taste with pepper, if using. Cover the dish with plastic wrap and refrigerate for 24 hours.

When ready to serve, remove the salmon from the refrigerator and cut into thin slices on the diagonal. The gravlax will keep for up to 4 days in the refrigerator.

SALMON GRAVLAX SUSHI

This sushi recipe doesn't require any complex or fiddly rolling techniques and is surprisingly simple to make. The cured salmon flavored with lemon and ginger makes a refreshing change from the usual raw salmon, but that's not to say it doesn't taste authentic, thanks to the seasoned sushi rice, potent wasabi paste and toasted nori sheets.

MAKES 20 PIECES   PREPARATION TIME: 20 MINUTES, PLUS STANDING, COOLING AND CHILLING   COOKING TIME: 10 MINUTES

1¼ cups plus 2 tablespoons sushi rice
2½ tablespoons rice wine vinegar
1 teaspoon sea salt
2½ teaspoons superfine sugar
½ recipe quantity Salmon Gravlax with
    Lemon & Ginger (see facing page),
    or smoked salmon, cut into thin slices

2 teaspoons wasabi paste
1¼ sheets toasted nori
Japanese soy sauce and pickled ginger,
    to serve

Cover the rice with water in a bowl and leave to stand for 20 minutes, then drain and rinse well. Transfer the rice to a pan and cover with 1¾ cups water. Bring to a boil, then turn down the heat to very low, cover and simmer for about 10 minutes until the water is absorbed. Remove the pan from the heat and leave the rice to stand, covered, for 10 minutes.

Mix together the rice wine vinegar, salt and sugar in a small bowl. Transfer the cooked rice to a large, shallow tray and spread it out evenly. Spoon the vinegar mixture over the rice and mix gently until the rice is coated. Leave the rice to cool.

Line a 9-inch pan with plastic wrap, leaving sufficient excess to fold over the top. Arrange the salmon slices, overlapping each other slightly, to cover the bottom of the lined pan. Put dots of the wasabi over the fish, then, using a wet knife, spread the rice in an even layer over the top. Press the rice down to make a firm layer.

Finish with a single layer of nori (you might need to cut the sheets with scissors to fit), then fold the surplus plastic wrap over the top to cover. Put a piece of cardboard on top and weight it down. Chill for 1 hour, then remove the weight and cardboard and, using a wet-bladed knife, cut into 20 equal pieces. Serve with soy sauce and pickled ginger.

SHELLFISH LINGUINE WITH CRISP CAPERS

A real treat of a dish made with a mixture of fresh clams and mussels. Choose small capers in brine packed in jars, and drain and rinse them well before use.

SERVES 4   PREPARATION TIME: 30 MINUTES   COOKING TIME: 15 MINUTES

3 pounds live mixed clams and mussels in the shell
2½ tablespoons olive oil
2 tablespoons small capers in brine, drained, rinsed and patted dry
12 ounces dried linguine
5 garlic cloves, finely chopped

5 large vine-ripened tomatoes, quartered, seeded and chopped
1 red chili, seeded and finely chopped
4 tablespoons chopped parsley leaves
1½ cups dry white wine
freshly ground black pepper

Discard any shellfish with broken shells or those that remain open when tapped. Scrub and clean the shellfish, pulling out the beard from the mussels. Rinse well in plenty of cold running water.

Heat 1½ teaspoons of the olive oil in a skillet and fry the capers for 2 to 3 minutes until crisp. Drain on paper towels and leave to one side. Bring a large saucepan of salted water to a boil and cook the linguine following the package directions until al dente. Drain the pasta and keep warm.

Meanwhile, heat the remaining olive oil in a large saucepan over medium heat. Add the garlic, tomatoes, chili and half of the parsley and cook, stirring, for 2 minutes. Pour in the wine and bring to a boil, then boil for 2 minutes, or until there is no longer an aroma of alcohol. Add the shellfish to the pan, cover and cook for 4 to 5 minutes, shaking the pan occasionally, until the shells open. Discard any that remain closed.

Remove half of the shellfish from their shells. Toss the pasta and the shelled shellfish into the pan and season to taste with black pepper; you are unlikely to need salt. Add the shellfish in their shells to the pan and serve immediately, sprinkled with the crisp capers and remaining parsley.

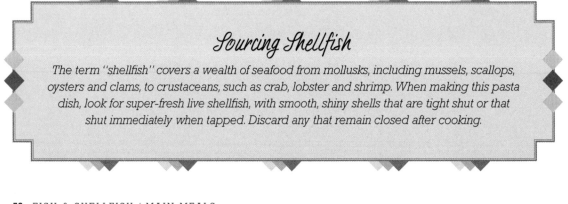

Sourcing Shellfish

The term "shellfish" covers a wealth of seafood from mollusks, including mussels, scallops, oysters and clams, to crustaceans, such as crab, lobster and shrimp. When making this pasta dish, look for super-fresh live shellfish, with smooth, shiny shells that are tight shut or that shut immediately when tapped. Discard any that remain closed after cooking.

Potted Shrimp

This is a traditional way to "preserve" tiny shrimp. Rock shrimp are suggested, but any very small shrimp can be used. Tiny shrimp are tiresomely fiddly to peel, so the recipe uses shelled shrimp. If you are starting from scratch you'll need about 1 pound 5 ounces shrimp in the shell.

SERVES 4   PREPARATION TIME: 15 MINUTES, PLUS CHILLING

½ cup butter
7 ounces cooked shelled rock shrimp or other very small shrimp
2 teaspoons lemon juice
¼ teaspoon ground mace
¼ teaspoon cayenne pepper
sea salt and freshly ground black pepper
thin slices of toast, to serve

Melt the butter in a small saucepan over medium-low heat. When it melts, add the shrimp and stir them in the butter for 30 seconds, then remove the pan from the heat.

Stir in the lemon juice, mace and cayenne and season to taste with salt. Add more seasoning to taste, if required. Using a slotted spoon, divide the shrimp among four ramekins, then pour the spiced butter over just to cover. Press the shrimp down into the melted butter slightly, then leave to cool.

Cover the potted shrimp with plastic wrap and transfer to the refrigerator to become firm. They can be kept refrigerated for up to 3 days. Remove from the refrigerator 30 minutes before serving, to let the butter soften slightly. Serve with thin slices of toast.

SEA BASS WITH **POTTED SHRIMP** IN BUTTER SAUCE

Sea bass is an excellent fish to use in this recipe, because its light, delicate flesh works well with the buttery, lemony sauce and the intense flavor of the tiny shrimp.

SERVES 4   PREPARATION TIME: 10 MINUTES   COOKING TIME: 5 MINUTES

4 sea bass fillets
all-purpose flour, for dusting
5 tablespoons butter
½ recipe quantity Potted Shrimp, about
   9 ounces (see facing page)

juice of 1 large lemon
sea salt and freshly ground black pepper
lemon wedges, boiled new potatoes and
   steamed spinach, to serve

Lightly dust the sea bass fillets with seasoned flour. Melt the butter in a large skillet over medium-high heat. When hot and sizzling, add the fish fillets, flesh-side down, and cook for 3 minutes, turning once, until slightly golden and almost cooked.

Add the potted shrimp and cook for 1 minute longer, spooning the buttery sauce over the fish.

Squeeze in the lemon juice and heat through briefly, continuing to spoon the sauce over the fish. Season to taste with salt and pepper and serve the fish with the potted shrimp sauce spooned over the top, with lemon wedges, new potatoes and spinach.

SPANISH STUFFED SQUID

Calasparra paella rice is ideal here, because its short grains readily take on the flavors of the vegetables, wine, stock and squid without losing their shape. It's important to cook the squid low and slow until so tender you can almost cut them with a fork.

SERVES 4   PREPARATION TIME: 30 MINUTES   COOKING TIME: 1½ HOURS

12 medium squid
a large pinch saffron threads
4 large vine-ripened tomatoes
2 tablespoons olive oil
1 large onion, chopped
1 romano or large red bell pepper,
   seeded and chopped
3 large garlic cloves, finely chopped

1¾ cups Calasparra paella rice
1 cup plus 2 tablespoons dry
   white wine
2¾ cups good-quality hot chicken stock
1 teaspoon mild smoked paprika
sea salt and freshly ground black pepper
chopped parsley leaves, for sprinkling

To prepare the squid, remove the intestines by pulling the tentacles and insides away from the body. Cut the tentacles just below the eyes and leave to one side for use in another dish. Discard the eyes and intestines. Pull out the plasticlike quill from the body cavity and discard. Rinse the body to remove any remaining entrails. Peel off any exterior browny-pink membrane, then rinse the squid again and leave to one side.

Soak the saffron threads in a little just-boiled water and leave to one side until needed.

Using a small, sharp knife, cut a shallow cross in the bottom of each tomato, then put them in a heatproof bowl and cover with just-boiled water. Leave to stand for 2 minutes, then drain. Peel off and discard the tomato skins, then seed and cut the flesh into large chunks. Strain the juices into a bowl.

Heat half of the olive oil in a large, heavy-bottomed skillet over medium heat. Cook the onion for 5 minutes, or until soft. Add the romano pepper and garlic and cook for 3 minutes longer, or until tender. Add the rice and stir until it is glossy. Pour in ⅔ cup of the wine, stir and cook until it is absorbed. Add half of the tomatoes, the saffron water, the stock and smoked paprika and stir until combined, then turn down the heat to low and simmer, stirring occasionally, for 20 minutes, or until the rice is just tender. Season well with salt and pepper.

Heat the oven to 350°F. Using a teaspoon, stuff the paella into the squid, pressing it down to the pointed tip (you want the squid to be as full as possible), then secure each with a wooden toothpick.

Put the squid in a large baking dish. Mix together the tomato juices, remaining diced tomato, olive oil, wine and 6 tablespoons water. Spoon this mixture over the squid and season to taste with salt and pepper. Cover the dish with foil and bake for 50 to 55 minutes until the squid is very tender. Serve the squid with the tomato-flavored juices spooned over the top, a twist of black pepper and a sprinkling of parsley.

VODKA-CURED SALMON

The salmon is cured briefly, just enough to give it a firm texture and good flavor, so this is a perfect recipe for a quick meal. Thick salmon fillets work best.

SERVES 4   PREPARATION TIME: 30 MINUTES, PLUS CHILLING   COOKING TIME: 5 MINUTES

¼ cup sea salt flakes
¼ cup sugar
4 thick salmon fillets, skin removed,
  about 6 ounces each
7 tablespoons vodka
2 tablespoons butter
2 teaspoons olive oil

½ cup crème fraîche or sour cream
juice of ½ lemon
freshly ground black pepper
samphire or green beans and crusty
  bread, to serve
Sweet Cucumber Relish (see page 21)
  or cucumber pickle, to serve

To prepare the salmon, mix together the salt and sugar in a bowl. Lay the salmon in a shallow dish and pour the vodka over. Spoon any vodka in the bottom of the dish over the fillets and repeat this a few times. Sprinkle the salt and sugar over the top of the salmon and rub it in until the salmon is evenly covered. Cover the dish with plastic wrap and chill for 2 hours.

Scrape the salt and sugar off the salmon fillets and rinse them briefly under cold running water. Pat them dry thoroughly with paper towels.

Heat the butter and olive oil in a large, nonstick skillet over medium heat. Season the salmon with pepper and cook for about 2 minutes on each side.

Meanwhile, mix together the crème fraîche and lemon juice and season to taste with pepper. Serve the salmon with the lemon-flavored crème fraîche spooned over the top, with the cucumber relish, samphire and crusty bread on the side.

Curing Fish

Before the days of refrigeration, curing was an essential method of preservation to extend the natural shelf life of fish, as well as a way of storing a glut of seafood. There are various methods of curing fish—salting, drying, smoking and pickling, or a combination of these techniques. For example, salmon is usually cured before being hot- or cold-smoked. Curing also influences the flavor and texture of seafood. When curing, use only the freshest seafood you can buy, ideally only specimens that smell pleasantly of the sea.

BLACKENED FISH WITH COUSCOUS & FRESH COCONUT RELISH

The coconut relish is full of fresh, zingy flavors and vibrant color, making it a perfect match for the crisp, spice-crusted fish. The relative blandness of the couscous is just the right foil for this flavor-packed dish. Use wholewheat couscous if you can find it.

SERVES 4   PREPARATION TIME: 30 MINUTES   COOKING TIME: 10 MINUTES

scant 1 cup wholewheat couscous or
  regular couscous
1 teaspoon vegetable bouillon powder
3 tablespoons butter
2 teaspoons ground coriander
1 teaspoon ground cumin
1 teaspoon sumac
1 teaspoon dried thyme
4 thick white fish fillets, about
  6 ounces each
1 tablespoon olive oil
sea salt and freshly ground black pepper

COCONUT RELISH:
4 tablespoons unsweetened shredded
  coconut
juice of 1 large lime
1 large handful mint leaves, roughly
  chopped
1 large handful cilantro leaves, roughly
  chopped
1 teaspoon sugar
1 green chili, seeded and finely chopped

To make the coconut relish, mix together all the ingredients in a nonmetallic bowl. Season to taste with salt and leave to one side to allow the flavors to mingle.

Put the couscous in a bowl and pour just-boiled over water to cover by ½ inch. Stir in the vegetable bouillon, powder, cover and leave for 5 minutes, or until the stock is absorbed. Using a fork, stir in 2 tablespoons of the butter, fluffing up the grains.

Meanwhile, mix together the ground coriander, cumin, sumac and thyme. Season to taste with salt and pepper and sprinkle the mixture over the flesh side of each fish fillet. Press the spices into the fish until evenly coated.

Heat the remaining butter with the olive oil in a large, nonstick skillet over medium heat. When the butter melts, add the fish, spice-side down first, and cook for about 2½ minutes on each side.

Serve the fish with the couscous and topped with a spoonful of the coconut relish.

Home-Smoked Trout

Home-smoking is immensely satisfying and surprisingly simple, because you don't need any special equipment. A wok with a lid is used here, but you can also use a heavy roasting pan or charcoal grill. The smoking mixture lends a subtle smokiness to the fish, which works particularly well with the delicate flavor of the trout.

SERVES 4   PREPARATION TIME: 15 MINUTES   COOKING TIME: 18 MINUTES

4 large trout fillets
vegetable oil, for greasing
salt and freshly ground black pepper

SMOKING MIXTURE:
3 large handfuls white rice
1 large handful Earl Grey tea leaves
2 tablespoons light brown sugar

Rinse the trout fillets and pat dry, then season to taste with salt and pepper.

To prepare the smoker, line the bottom and lid of the wok with aluminum foil. Put the wok on a wok stand, if you have one. Mix together the rice, tea leaves and sugar in the wok. Lightly oil a wire rack and position it above the smoking mixture, making sure it does not touch the mixture.

Put the trout, skin side-down, on the rack and cover with the foil-lined lid.

Heat the wok over medium heat until you start to see little wisps of smoke escaping around the lid. Carefully patch up any leaks with foil, turn down the heat to medium-low and make sure the kitchen is well ventilated. Smoke the trout for 18 minutes, or until the flesh is opaque. Make sure the mixture in the wok continues to smoke during this time. Remove from the heat and, when the smoke subsides, remove the lid. Using a pancake turner or metal spatula, transfer the trout to serving plates.

SMOKED TROUT WITH POTATO LATKES & BEET RELISH

Inspired by Jewish cuisine, the lightly smoked, delicate fillets of trout are perfect with the crisp, golden potato latkes and slightly sweet roasted beets coated in a horseradish cream sauce.

SERVES 4   PREPARATION TIME: 20 MINUTES   COOKING TIME: 55 MINUTES

1 recipe quantity Home-Smoked Trout
  (see page 68)
arugula, spinach and watercress leaves,
  to serve

BEET RELISH:
14 ounces uncooked beets, washed,
  roots trimmed and quartered
1 teaspoon olive oil
½ cup crème fraîche or sour cream
2 tablespoons lemon juice
2 tablespoons horseradish sauce

1 tablespoon chopped dill, for sprinkling
sea salt and freshly ground black pepper

POTATO LATKES:
1 pound 10 ounces Idaho or other baking
  potatoes, peeled
5 tablespoons all-purpose flour
1 teaspoon baking powder
1 teaspoon salt
2 eggs, lightly beaten
3 to 4 tablespoons olive oil

Heat the oven to 350°F. Line two baking sheets with a double layer of paper towels. To make the beet relish, cook the beets in a pan of boiling water for 20 minutes, or until soft but not cooked through. Transfer the beets to a roasting pan. Drizzle the olive oil over them and turn until they are coated. Season to taste with salt and pepper. Roast for 30 to 35 minutes until tender and the skin is crinkled and slightly caramelized.

While the beets are roasting, grate the potatoes in a food processor or with a box grater—ideally, you want long, thin strands of potato. Transfer the potatoes to a clean dish towel or a piece of cheesecloth and wring out as much liquid as possible.

Mix together the flour, baking powder and salt in a large bowl. Season to taste with pepper and add the potatoes. Stir until the potatoes are evenly coated in the flour mixture, then add the eggs and mix again.

Heat 3 tablespoons of olive oil in a large, heavy-based skillet over medium heat. Take a small handful of the potato mixture, letting the eggy batter drain off a little, and put it into the pan. Flatten slightly with a metal spatula into a rough-edged 3-inch circle, then repeat so you have 3 or 4 latkes in the pan. Fry them for 3 to 4 minutes on each side until golden and crisp. Transfer the latkes to a prepared baking sheet and keep warm in the oven while you cook the remaining latkes. The mixture will make 8 latkes in total.

When the beets are cooked, remove them from the oven. Rub off some of the skin if it is loose (you don't need to remove it all) and cut the beets into small pieces. Mix together the crème fraîche, lemon juice and horseradish in a bowl. Season to taste with salt and pepper, then stir in the beets. Sprinkle the dill over the top. Cut the smoked trout into bite-size pieces and serve with the potato latkes, a good spoonful of the beet relish and some arugula, spinach and watercress leaves.

3. Cheese
&
Dairy

BUFFALO MOZZARELLA & SALAMI BRUSCHETTA WITH BASIL OIL

Buffalo mozzarella is perfect here, because its fresh, slightly sour, milky flavor and soft texture temper the piquant saltiness of the cured, air-dried salami. The success of this recipe lies almost exclusively with the quality of the ingredients, so choose the best you can afford and you'll be rewarded with great-tasting bruschetta.

SERVES 4   PREPARATION TIME: 20 MINUTES   COOKING TIME: 20 MINUTES

8 thick slices country-style bread
2 large garlic cloves, halved
olive oil, for brushing
9 ounces buffalo mozzarella cheese,
    drained, patted dry and sliced
16 thin slices salami of your choice,
    casings removed
6 large vine-ripened tomatoes,
    quartered, seeded and diced

BASIL OIL:
2 large handfuls basil leaves, plus extra
    for sprinkling
1 garlic clove, crushed
juice of ½ lemon
6 tablespoons extra virgin olive oil
sea salt and freshly ground black pepper

Heat a large cast-iron, ridged grill pan over high heat. Grill the bread, 2 or 3 slices at a time, until both sides are toasted and lightly charred in places.

Meanwhile, make the basil oil. Blend together the basil, garlic, lemon juice and extra virgin olive oil in a mini food processor until combined. Season to taste with salt and pepper and leave to one side.

Rub the cut side of the garlic over the toasted bread, then brush with a little olive oil. Top with mozzarella, salami and tomatoes. Season and drizzle over some basil oil. Serve sprinkled with basil leaves.

Mozzarella

In Italy, delis and supermarkets proudly display large, open containers of fresh mozzarella in all shapes and sizes, from the smallest bocconcini to the most-prized burrata and mozzarella di bufala. While most mozzarella is now made from cow's milk, it is still possible to buy the traditional buffalo milk alternative. This fresh, unripened cheese is the classic pizza topping, but it's also great in salads, such as insalata caprese. Scamorza and the smoked version, scamorza affumicata, belong to the same family as mozzarella. It has an unusual pear shape and a slightly firmer, drier texture than mozzarella. Burrata is also worth trying in this recipe. This rich, indulgent cheese has an outer shell of mozzarella with a creamy interior—delicious!

CORNISH BLUE, BACON & CARAMELIZED APPLE SALAD

Multi-award-winning Cornish Blue is a relatively new British cheese that is making its mark with cheese aficionados. This young blue cheese combines wonderfully with the sticky golden apple slices and toasted walnuts in this recipe. If you can't find Cornish Blue, French Roquefort or Italian Dolcelatte are great alternatives.

SERVES 4   PREPARATION TIME: 20 MINUTES   COOKING TIME: 20 MINUTES

½ cup walnut halves
2 tablespoons butter
2 firm, crisp apples, peeled, cored and sliced into wedges
1 tablespoon honey
9 ounces thick-cut bacon, cut into ¼-inch lardons
6 cups watercress, tough stems removed
5 ounces Cornish Blue cheese, or other blue cheese of choice, cut or crumbled into bite-size chunks

DRESSING:
5 tablespoons extra virgin olive oil
2 tablespoons lemon juice
1 teaspoon Dijon mustard
sea salt and fresh ground black pepper

Mix together the ingredients for the dressing, seasoning lightly with salt and more generously with pepper (the bacon and blue cheese will be very salty). Leave to one side.

Toast the walnuts in a large, dry skillet for 2 to 3 minutes on each side until starting to color. Remove the walnuts from the pan and leave to cool.

Melt the butter in the skillet. Add the apple wedges and cook for 5 minutes, turning once. Stir in the honey, turn the apples to coat them in the buttery honey sauce and cook for 1 minute longer, or until golden. Remove the apple slices from the pan and leave to one side.

Wipe the pan clean, then add the bacon and cook over low heat until the fat begins to run. Turn up the heat slightly and fry the bacon for 6 to 8 minutes until golden and crisp. Remove the bacon from the pan with a slotted spoon and drain on paper towels.

Spoon as much of the dressing over the watercress as needed to coat the leaves. Toss until combined, then scatter the walnuts, bacon, cheese and apples over the top.

Labneh

This Middle Eastern drained yogurt cheese is similar in consistency to a thick cream cheese. Easy to make at home, labneh is the perfect starting point for burgeoning cheesemakers. Use good-quality Greek yogurt or thick plain yogurt for the best flavor and texture. Here, walnut-size balls of labneh are stored in an herb-flavored olive oil, but there are many variations, both sweet and savory, that are worth experimenting with. You'll find some ideas below.

MAKES 16 WALNUT-SIZE BALLS   PREPARATION TIME: 30 MINUTES, PLUS AT LEAST 12 HOURS DRAINING

2 cups plus 2 tablespoons good-quality Greek yogurt or thick plain yogurt
1½ teaspoons sea salt
4 oregano or marjoram sprigs
4 thyme sprigs
extra virgin olive oil, to cover

Rest a strainer over a mixing bowl and line with a piece of cheesecloth or a clean kitchen cloth.

Mix the yogurt with the salt and spoon it into the cloth-lined strainer. Pull the cloth up around the yogurt and twist the top to make a bundle. Leave the yogurt to drain in the refrigerator for 12 hours and preferably up to 24 hours; the longer you leave it the firmer the labneh will be. Give the bundle a gentle squeeze every so often to encourage any whey to drain away.

Remove the cheesecloth bundle from the strainer and open it to reveal a smooth, thick soft cheese. The labneh is ready to eat now, or can be formed into balls and stored in olive oil.

To store in olive oil, roll the labneh into 16 equal, walnut-size balls. Put them in a large sterilized jar, add the herbs and pour over enough olive oil to cover. Cover and store in the refrigerator for up to 1 week.

VARIATIONS
• Add sun-dried tomatoes, chilies or whole spices such as coriander to the jar.
• Roll the balls of labneh in chopped fresh herbs mixed with a little chopped red chili until coated before putting them in the jar. Try experimenting with ground spices, too.
• Tip the labneh out of the cheesecloth onto a serving plate after draining. Drizzle with good-quality honey and scatter a handful of roughly chopped toasted walnuts over the top. Serve with fresh ripe figs or peach slices.

LABNEH & LAMB FLATBREADS WITH MINT SALSA

With a marinade and mint salsa packed with the bold flavors and vibrant colors of North Africa, the balls of labneh add a touch of calm with their soothing, creamy, slightly acidic taste.

**SERVES 4   PREPARATION TIME: 30 MINUTES, PLUS MARINATING
COOKING TIME: 10 MINUTES**

18 ounces boneless lamb loins or
    boneless loin chops
4 Middle Eastern flatbreads, warmed
2 handfuls baby spinach leaves
½ recipe quantity Labneh (see facing
    page) or 1⅓ cups crumbled feta cheese
sea salt and freshly ground black pepper

MARINADE:
2 teaspoons dried mint
2 teaspoons ground cumin
4 teaspoons ground coriander
½ teaspoon cayenne pepper
3 tablespoons olive oil
1 tablespoon lemon juice

MINT SALSA:
5 large vine-ripened tomatoes, quartered,
    seeded and diced
½ small red onion, finely chopped
heaped 1 tablespoon chopped peppadew
    chilies, drained
1 large handful mint leaves, roughly
    chopped
2 tablespoons extra virgin olive oil
juice of ½ lemon

Mix together all the ingredients for the marinade in a large, shallow nonmetallic dish. Add the lamb to the dish and spoon the marinade over until the meat is well coated. Season the lamb to taste with salt and pepper, then leave to marinate for 1 hour, covered.

Meanwhile, mix together the ingredients for the mint salsa in a nonmetallic serving bowl. Season to taste with salt and pepper to taste. Leave at room temperature until ready to serve.

Heat a large cast-iron, ridged grill pan over high heat. Grill the lamb for 5 minutes, or until cooked to your liking, turning once; it should still be pink in the middle. You might need to cook the lamb in batches. Transfer the lamb to a plate, cover with foil and leave to rest for 5 minutes. Cut the lamb into long slices.

To serve, top the warm flatbreads with the spinach and lamb. Crumble the labneh on top and let everyone help themselves to the mint salsa at the table.

CRISP MANCHEGO WITH CHORIZO-SPIKED RATATOUILLE

The chorizo gives a real kick to this vibrantly colored ratatouille, similar to the Spanish pisto. The Manchego slices are fried in breadcrumbs to give them a crisp, golden coating.

SERVES 4   PREPARATION TIME: 25 MINUTES   COOKING TIME: 25 MINUTES

¼ cup plus 1 tablespoon all-purpose flour
2 eggs, beaten
heaped 1 cup fresh bread crumbs
9 ounces Manchego cheese, rind removed, and cut into 12 fingers
7 tablespoons vegetable oil

CHORIZO-SPIKED RATATOUILLE:
2 tablespoons olive oil
1 large onion, sliced
1 teaspoon dried oregano

3 cloves garlic, finely chopped
1 red and 1 yellow bell pepper, seeded and cut into bite-size pieces
1 cup roughly chopped fresh chorizo
6 small zucchini, sliced
4 large vine-ripened tomatoes, seeded and roughly chopped
1 handful parsley, leaves chopped
1 handful basil, leaves torn
⅓ cup black olives
sea salt and freshly ground black pepper

First make the chorizo-spiked ratatouille. Heat the olive oil in a large, heavy-bottomed saucepan and fry the onion for 8 minutes, or until soft. Add the oregano, garlic, red and yellow peppers, chorizo and zucchini and fry, stirring occasionally, for 3 to 4 minutes longer until the vegetables are soft. Add the tomatoes and cook for 5 minutes, or until they break down slightly to make a sauce, then stir in the herbs and olives. Season to taste with salt and pepper. Cover the pan and keep warm while you prepare the Manchego.

Put the flour, eggs and bread crumbs into three separate shallow bowls. Dip each stick of Manchego into the beaten egg, followed by the flour, then in the egg again and finally the bread crumbs until coated.

Heat the vegetable oil in a deep skillet over medium heat. Fry the crumbed Manchego sticks, in three batches, for about 1 minute on each side until crisp and golden. Drain on paper towels. Serve the ratatouille topped with the crisp Manchego.

Manchego

Manchego is probably Spain's best-known cheese. It is produced all over the country, but the true Manchego is made from the milk of the Manchego sheep from the La Mancha region. It has a good depth of flavor, with a buttery, nutty taste and a firm, slightly crumbly texture.

BAKED FETA & SHRIMP WITH CHERMOULA

Baking does great things to feta, tempering its saltiness and giving it a much smoother, creamier texture. Serve the feta with the baked shrimp in the middle of the table and let everyone help themselves, shelling and dunking the shrimp into the Moroccan chermoula. This fragrant, spicy, herby concoction is traditionally used as a marinade, but it's just as good as a sauce or dip.

SERVES 4   PREPARATION TIME: 25 MINUTES   COOKING TIME: 18 MINUTES

14-ounce block feta cheese, drained and
   patted dry
4 tablespoons extra virgin olive oil
3 oregano sprigs
3 thyme sprigs
½ teaspoon dried mint
4 garlic cloves, sliced
1 pound raw large shrimp in shell
a large pinch dried chili flakes
3 tablespoons white wine
sea salt and freshly ground black pepper
crusty bread and green salad, to serve

CHERMOULA:
2 handfuls cilantro, leaves chopped
2 handfuls flat-leaf parsley, leaves
   chopped
2 garlic cloves, finely chopped
1 teaspoon harissa paste
1 red chili, seeded and finely chopped
1 teaspoon ground cumin
1 teaspoon ground coriander
juice of 1 large lemon
4 tablespoons extra virgin olive oil

Heat the oven to 400°F. To make the chermoula, mix together all the ingredients in a bowl and season to taste with salt and pepper. Leave to one side to let the flavors mingle.

Lay a piece of foil large enough to wrap the feta on a large baking sheet. Put the feta in the middle of the foil and pour 2 tablespoons of the olive oil over, then top with the oregano, thyme, mint and 1 of the sliced garlic cloves. Season with pepper to taste. Bring up the sides of the foil and scrunch the top to make a loose package. Place in the oven and bake for 15 to 18 minutes until soft.

Meanwhile, put the shrimp in a large baking dish with the remaining sliced garlic, the chili flakes, the remaining olive oil and the white wine. Season to taste with salt and bake for 8 to 10 minutes, basting the shrimp occasionally with the juices in the dish, until they turn pink and are cooked through.

Transfer the feta to a plate and serve in slices with the shrimp and their cooking juices and the chermoula, with crusty bread and a green salad on the side.

TWICE-BAKED CHEESE SOUFFLÉS WITH PEAR & RED LEAF SALAD

These soufflés can be made the day before serving them. The best thing about baking them twice is that you don't need to worry whether they will rise; magically, they rise again when baked for the second time. Be warned, though—they are rich and very delectable!

SERVES 4   PREPARATION TIME: 30 MINUTES, PLUS INFUSING AND COOLING
  COOKING TIME: 45 MINUTES

¾ cup plus 2 tablespoons whole milk
1 bay leaf
1 large garlic clove, halved
3½ tablespoons butter
3½ tablespoons all-purpose flour
2 teaspoons Dijon mustard
scant 1 cup shredded sharp cheddar
  cheese
scant ½ cup grated aged Gruyère cheese
3 eggs, separated
4 tablespoons double cream

PEAR AND RED LEAF SALAD:
8 red leaf lettuce leaves, torn
⅔ cup shredded red cabbage
2 crisp but ripe pears, cored and
  sliced lengthwise, then tossed
  in a little lemon juice
2 tablespoons extra virgin olive oil
1 tablespoon lemon juice
2 tablespoons snipped chives
sea salt and freshly ground black pepper

Warm the milk in a small saucepan with the bay leaf and garlic. Remove from the heat and leave the milk to infuse for 30 minutes. Reheat just before using. Heat the oven to 400°F and put a baking sheet inside to heat. Melt the butter in a saucepan and use a little to grease four ¾-cup ramekins.

Add the flour to the remaining melted butter in the pan and stir to make a roux. Cook over medium heat for 1 minute, stirring. Remove the bay leaf and garlic from the warm milk and gradually stir it into the roux. Bring to a boil, then turn down the heat and simmer, stirring, for 5 minutes, or until thick and smooth.

Pour the sauce into a bowl and stir in the mustard, cheddar and 2 tablespoons of the Gruyère. Beat in the egg yolks, one at a time. In a separate large bowl, beat the egg whites until they form stiff peaks. Using a large spoon, fold the whites into the cheese mixture in three batches. Spoon the mixture into the ramekins.

Put the ramekins on the hot baking sheet and bake for 18 to 20 minutes until risen. Leave to cool, then run a knife around the edge of the soufflés and carefully unmold them, upside down, onto a plate. Keep in the refrigerator until ready to bake the second time.

To serve, heat the oven to 425°F. Put the soufflés on a baking sheet, then spoon 1 tablespoon of the cream and the remaining Gruyère over each one. Bake for 10 to 12 minutes until risen and the cheese melts.

Meanwhile, to make the salad, put the lettuce, red cabbage and pears in a serving bowl. Beat together the olive oil and lemon juice and season to taste with salt and pepper. Spoon this dressing over the salad and toss until combined. Scatter the chives over the top. Serve the soufflés with the salad.

HALLOUMI, FIG & ALMOND SALAD

The sweet succulence of the fig makes it a great match for salty, firm halloumi cheese in this salad. When buying figs, look for ripe fruits that yield slightly when pressed gently, because these will have the best flavor. Figs don't ripen after picking, so avoid fruit that is too firm—it will be lacking in sweetness. Plan to make this salad just before serving, because halloumi is at its best when still warm and softened by the heat.

SERVES 4 PREPARATION TIME: 15 MINUTES COOKING TIME: 10 MINUTES

½ cup blanched almonds
2 handfuls arugula leaves
2 handfuls pea shoots
6 figs, quartered
1 tablespoon olive oil
9 ounces halloumi cheese, drained,
    patted dry and cubed
5 mint sprigs, leaves torn

DRESSING:
4 tablespoons extra virgin olive oil
1 tablespoon red wine vinegar
1 teaspoon honey
½ teaspoon Dijon mustard
sea salt and freshly ground black pepper

Mix together all the ingredients for the dressing, seasoning to taste with salt and pepper.

Toast the almonds in a large, dry skillet over medium heat for about 5 minutes, turning once, until they are light brown. Remove from the pan and leave to cool.

Meanwhile, put the arugula, pea shoots and figs in a large serving bowl. Scatter the almonds over the salad.

Heat the oil in the skillet and cook the halloumi for about 5 minutes, turning occasionally, until soft and just golden in places. Scatter the halloumi over the salad. Spoon as much of the dressing over the top as required and toss until everything is coated and combined. Sprinkle the mint over before serving.

Halloumi Cheese

A traditional sheep- and goat-milk cheese from Cyprus, halloumi has a high melting point, so it holds its shape when heated. You don't want to heat it for too long, though, because it becomes tough and rubbery—it needs just long enough to soften and take on a light golden crust. It's definitely best served warm. Always pat halloumi dry with paper towels before cooking—this makes sure it becomes crisp and golden, rather than soggy and water-logged.

Homemade Buttermilk

At first I wasn't sure about including this recipe for buttermilk, because it's so very simple. But I decided to include it because it isn't always easy to buy, and it makes a versatile and useful addition to a cook's repertoire. Once a by-product of buttermaking, buttermilk was the liquid left in the churn after the butter formed. It has a slightly sour, acidic taste and is usually used in baking. Biscuits, pancakes, soda bread and cakes all benefit from the addition of buttermilk. So, too, does a marinade for meat or poultry (see facing page), because buttermilk improves the texture of meat and makes it incredibly tender. This recipe produces a rich buttermilk that's equivalent to traditional versions, but you can replace the whole milk with low-fat milk and omit the cream if you'd rather.

MAKES ABOUT 1⅓ CUPS   PREPARATION TIME: 5 MINUTES, PLUS STANDING

1¼ cups whole milk
4 teaspoons lemon juice or distilled vinegar
1 tablespoon heavy cream (optional)

Pour the milk into a large measuring jug and stir in the lemon juice. Leave to stand at room temperature for about 20 minutes until it starts to curdle. Stir in the cream, if using. Stir well before use, then use as required in your recipe.

Stir the buttermilk again before using. It will keep, covered, in the refrigerator for up to 2 days.

BUTTERMILK ROAST CHICKEN

Buttermilk makes a surprisingly good marinade for chicken, because it makes it tender and moist. Serve with roasted new potatoes and an arugula salad.

**SERVES 4   PREPARATION TIME: 15 MINUTES, PLUS MARINATING AND RESTING
COOKING TIME: 1 HOUR 10 MINUTES**

¾ recipe quantity Homemade Buttermilk
  (see facing page)
4 garlic cloves, halved lengthwise
1 tablespoon sea salt
1 tablespoon honey
1 tablespoon Dijon mustard

1 teaspoon paprika, plus extra
  for sprinkling
1 chicken, about 3 pounds 5 ounces
1 teaspoon olive oil
freshly ground black pepper
roast new potatoes, arugula salad and
  Mayonnaise (see page 126), to serve

Mix together the buttermilk, garlic, salt, honey, mustard and paprika in a bowl and season with pepper. Put the chicken in a large ziplock bag, pour in the marinade and seal. Turn the chicken to coat it with the marinade. Put the bag in a bowl and marinate in the refrigerator for up to 24 hours, turning the chicken occasionally.

Heat the oven to 375°F. Remove the chicken from the bag and put it in a foil-lined roasting pan. Discard the marinade. Drizzle the oil over and season with more paprika, salt and pepper. Roast, basting occasionally, for 1 hour 10 minutes, or until the chicken is cooked through. Cover the chicken with foil to keep it warm and leave to rest for 15 minutes before serving with roasted new potatoes, arugula salad and mayonnaise.

SLOW-COOKED PORK IN MILK

Inspired by the Italian dish arista al latte, the pork steaks here are slow-cooked in milk and infused with lemon, oregano and garlic. The milk keeps the meat moist and has a tenderizing effect, and it cooks down to a light, fragrant sauce. The pork is delicious served with crisp roast potatoes, steamed zucchini and long-stem broccoli.

SERVES 4   PREPARATION TIME: 20 MINUTES   COOKING TIME: 2 HOURS 5 MINUTES

4 rindless pork shoulder steaks or blade steaks, about ½ pound each
1 tablespoon olive oil
2 tablespoons butter
3 garlic cloves, sliced
5 oregano sprigs, plus 1 tablespoon leaves for sprinkling

2½ cups whole milk
4 strips pared lemon zest
2 bay leaves
sea salt and freshly ground black pepper
roast potatoes, green vegetables and lemon wedges, to serve

Season both sides of each pork steak to taste with salt and pepper. Heat the oil in a large Dutch oven over medium-high heat and sear the pork in two batches until brown on both sides. Remove the pork from the pot and leave to one side.

Turn down the heat slightly, then add the butter and melt it. Add the garlic and oregano sprigs. Return the pork to the pot, pour the milk over and tuck the lemon zest and bay leaves between the steaks.

Bring the milk to a boil, then turn down the heat to very low and simmer the pork, partially covered, for 45 minutes. Turn the steaks in the milk after 20 minutes. The liquid should simmer very gently all the time so the milk reduces gradually and the pork cooks slowly.

Remove the lid and simmer the pork for 45 minutes longer. The milk will curdle, but this is normal. Using a metal spatula, remove the pork and leave it to rest, covered with foil, for 5 minutes.

Season the sauce to taste with salt and pepper and bring to a boil, then gently bubble away for 5 minutes, or until it reduces by one-third and is almost caramel in color. Strain and discard the solids.

Serve the pork with the sauce spooned over the top and sprinkled with extra oregano, with roast potatoes, green vegetables and lemon wedges for squeezing over.

TARTIFLETTE

Winter food at its best, this comforting potato, bacon and cheese gratin originates from the Haute-Savoie region of France. It is traditionally made with Reblochon, a cow's-milk cheese with a slightly nutty flavor, soft interior and pinkish-brown rind. Serve with charcuterie and pickled onions and gherkins.

**SERVES 4 (SERVES 6 AS A SIDE DISH)   PREPARATION TIME: 15 MINUTES
   COOKING TIME: 50 MINUTES**

2¼ pounds small salad potatoes
1 teaspoon olive oil
7 ounces thick-cut bacon, cut into
   ¼-inch lardons
1 onion, roughly chopped
3 garlic cloves, roughly chopped
scant ½ cup dry white wine

¾ cup plus 2 tablespoons heavy cream
12 ounces Reblochon cheese, rind
   removed and sliced
sea salt and freshly ground black pepper
charcuterie, pickled onions and gherkins,
   to serve

Heat the oven to 400°F. Cook the potatoes in a pan of boiling salted water for 10 to 15 minutes until tender. Drain and leave to one side until cool enough to handle.

Meanwhile, put the olive oil and bacon in a nonstick skillet over low heat and heat until the fat starts to render from the lardons. Turn up the heat to medium, add the onion and fry, stirring occasionally, for 5 to 6 minutes until the onion is soft and the lardons are crisp. Add the garlic and cook for 1 minute longer.

Pour in the wine and stir well to remove any sticky brown bits on the bottom of the pan, then continue to cook until most of the wine evaporates.

Slice the potatoes and gently mix with the lardon mixture in a baking dish. Pour the cream over the top and season to taste with pepper (you are unlikely to need more salt). Lay the cheese top and bake for 20 minutes, or until the cheese melts and is golden in places. Serve with charcuterie, pickled onions and gherkins.

Washed-Rind Cheese

Reblochon is the traditional cheese for tartiflette, but if you can't get hold of it try another washed-rind cheese, such as Époisses, Taleggio or fontina, which all have a similar sweet, nutty, earthy flavor and are good to cook with because they have excellent melting qualities. I prefer to remove the hard rind before use, but this is a personal choice.

STEAK WITH DOLCELATTE SAUCE & BALSAMIC TOMATOES

Here, blue-veined Dolcelatte cheese melts to make a creamy, slightly sweet sauce for steak. The rich sauce is best served in small amounts on the side, rather than being poured over the meat. Take the steak out of the refrigerator an hour before you intend to cook it so it comes to room temperature, and pat it dry to remove any excess moisture.

SERVES 4   PREPARATION TIME: 20 MINUTES   COOKING TIME: 20 MINUTES

4 filet mignons, about 7 ounces each,
  at room temperature, patted dry
1 tablespoon olive oil
sea salt and freshly ground black pepper
crusty bread, to serve

BALSAMIC TOMATOES:
3 tablespoons olive oil
12 ounces cherry tomatoes, halved

4 thyme sprigs, leaves removed
2 tablespoons balsamic vinegar

DOLCELATTE SAUCE:
4 tablespoons dry white wine
5 ounces Dolcelatte cheese, rind removed
  and cut into pieces
⅔ cup crème fraîche or sour cream

To make the balsamic tomatoes, heat the olive oil in a skillet over medium-low heat. Add the tomatoes and half of the thyme, then cook for 1 minute. Turn the tomatoes over and pour in the balsamic vinegar. Cook for 2 minutes longer, or until the balsamic vinegar reduces and the tomatoes start to caramelize. Season to taste with salt and pepper, then leave to one side.

Rub the steaks with a little olive oil, then season on each side with salt and pepper.

Heat a large cast-iron, ridged grill pan or skillet over high heat. Add the steaks, then turn down the heat to medium and cook for 5 to 6 minutes, turning the steaks twice and occasionally pressing the meat onto the pan. (You might need to cook the steaks in two batches, depending on the size of your pan.) After this time the steaks should be seared on the outside and medium-rare in the middle. Transfer them to a warm plate and leave to rest, covered with foil, for 5 minutes.

To make the Dolcelatte sauce, add the wine to the pan with any juices from the resting steaks. Stir to release any bits stuck to the bottom of the pan and simmer until the wine has reduced by half. If you've used a grill pan, pour the wine into a saucepan. Add the Dolcelatte and crème fraîche. Heat through, stirring, until the cheese melts, then season to taste with pepper.

Serve each steak with a generous spoonful of the Dolcelatte sauce and the tomatoes, sprinkled with the remaining thyme, and with crusty bread on the side.

Homemade Crème Fraîche

Velvety, slightly nutty and with a gentle tang, crème fraîche lends a smooth, mellow creaminess to savory sauces, or a spoonful curbs the sweetness of a cake or dessert. Crème fraîche is similar to sour cream, but has a thicker texture and is not quite as tangy. It is more stable, too, resisting curdling and separation when heated, which makes it ideal in cooking. While crème fraîche is available commercially, there's nothing like making your own and it takes very little effort.

**MAKES ABOUT 1¼ CUPS   PREPARATION TIME: 10 MINUTES,
PLUS UP TO 24 HOURS STANDING**

1¼ cups heavy cream
2 tablespoons buttermilk

Pour the cream into a saucepan and slowly warm it over medium-low heat until it reaches 105°F on a thermometer. Remove the pan from the heat and pour the cream into a sterilized glass jar. Stir in the buttermilk until combined, then cover with plastic wrap or parchment paper and secure with a rubber band.

Put the jar in a warm, draft-free place. Leave until the crème fraîche becomes thick, which can take anywhere from 12 to 24 hours. Once thick, stir well, then cover with a lid and chill. The crème fraîche is ready to eat now, but will continue to thicken. Store in the refrigerator for up to 2 weeks.

SALMON, LEEK & **CRÈME FRAÎCHE** BRAID

This is an ideal summer alternative to roast meat for a family meal. The salmon fillet is encased in a layer of creamy leeks and puff pastry, then baked until flaky and golden. Buy a middle-cut piece of salmon fillet—it's likely to be of an even thickness so the fish cooks evenly.

SERVES 6   PREPARATION TIME: 30 MINUTES   COOKING TIME: 45 MINUTES

butter, for greasing
2 leeks, finely chopped
1 large handful watercress, roughly
   chopped
½ recipe quantity Homemade Crème
   Fraîche (see facing page), about ⅔ cup
1 salmon fillet, about 1½ pounds, skinned
13 ounces puff pastry dough sheets,
   thawed if frozen

all-purpose flour, for dusting
1 egg yolk, lightly beaten
sea salt and freshly ground black pepper
new potatoes and green beans, to serve

CHIVE AND LEMON MAYONNAISE:
7 tablespoons Mayonnaise (see page 126)
juice of ½ lemon
1 tablespoon snipped chives

Heat the oven to 400°F and lightly grease a large cookie sheet with butter.

Steam the leeks for 5 minutes, or until tender. Remove them from the heat and leave until they are cool enough to handle, then, using your hands, squeeze out as much water as possible. This will prevent them from making the dough soggy during baking. Put the leeks in a mixing bowl and stir in the watercress and crème fraîche. Season to taste with salt and pepper.

Using a pair of tweezers, remove any pin bones from the salmon and pat it dry with paper towels.

Lay the pastry dough on a lightly floured countertop and roll out slightly to make a large rectangle that will enclose the salmon. Lay the salmon down the middle of the dough rectangle. Spoon the leek mixture over the top in an even layer.

Make diagonal cuts in the dough down both sides of the salmon to make even-size strips. Cut away the corners of the rectangle (this makes the dough easier to braid). Fold the ends of the dough over the salmon, then "braid" the strips: take the top strip from the left side and fold it over the salmon, then take the top strip from the right side and fold it over the first strip. Continue until you have completely covered the salmon with alternating crossed-over strips.

Using two spatulas, carefully transfer the salmon to the prepared cookie sheet. Brush the dough with the egg yolk. Bake for 35 to 40 minutes until the pastry is golden and the salmon is cooked through.

Meanwhile, mix together the mayonnaise and lemon juice. Add 1 tablespoon water to loosen the mixture, then scatter the chives over the top. Serve the salmon braid in slices with a spoonful of the mayonnaise, and new potatoes and green beans.

SMOKED HADDOCK WITH TALEGGIO SAUCE

The northern Italian cheese Taleggio (see page 91), with its semisoft texture and slightly fruity flavor, melts into a wonderfully rich and creamy sauce with a robust aroma. Served with smoked haddock and a poached egg, this is the most heart-warming combination.

SERVES 4   PREPARATION TIME: 15 MINUTES   COOKING TIME: 20 MINUTES

4 thick, undyed smoked haddock fillets
   (finnan haddie), about 6 ounces each
1 teaspoon olive oil
½ lemon, cut into 4 slices
4 extra-large eggs
10 ounces Swiss chard or spinach
freshly ground black pepper
crusty bread, to serve

TALEGGIO SAUCE
1 cup dry white wine
6 ounces Taleggio cheese, rind removed
   and cut into pieces
1 teaspoon cornstarch, mixed with
   1 teaspoon whole milk
1 tablespoon heavy cream

Heat the oven to 375°F. Lay a piece of foil large enough to make a package for the haddock fillets on a baking sheet and lightly grease with the olive oil. Put the haddock fillets on the foil, side by side, and season to taste with pepper. Lay a slice of lemon on top of each fillet. Bring up the sides of the foil and scrunch the top together to make a loose package. Put the baking sheet in the oven and bake for 15 to 20 minutes, depending on the thickness of the fillets, until they are opaque.

About 5 minutes after putting the haddock in the oven, poach the eggs. Put a large, deep skillet on the stovetop and fill with about 1 inch just-boiled water. Keeping the heat low, break the eggs, one at a time, into a teacup, then slip them into the just-simmering water. Cook the eggs for 1 minute, then remove the pan from the heat and let the eggs sit in the hot water for 10 minutes, or until the whites are cooked and set but the yolks are still slightly runny.

To make the Taleggio sauce, pour the wine into a small pan and bring to a boil. Turn down the heat to medium-low and let the wine bubble away until reduced by one-third and there is no longer any aroma of alcohol. Stir in the Taleggio until it melts, then add the cornstarch mixture. Cook for about 3 minutes, stirring, until the sauce is thick enough to coat the back of the spoon. Stir in the heavy cream, cover the pan and leave to one side.

Steam the chard for 3 minutes, or until it wilts.

To serve, divide the chard among four bowls. Remove the haddock from its foil package and put on top of the chard. Using a slotted spoon, lift the eggs out of the water, one at a time, and drain briefly on paper towels. Put an egg on each haddock fillet and spoon the sauce over. Season to taste with pepper before serving with crusty bread.

HERB & RICOTTA CHEESECAKE WITH ROASTED TOMATO PESTO

The delicate freshness of ricotta cheese is the perfect foundation for this light, savory cheesecake. Boosted by the rich, earthy flavor of Parmesan and a smattering of fresh herbs, the cheesecake is served with a vibrant tomato pesto. Look for the most flavorsome tomatoes you can find and a good fruity olive oil.

SERVES 6 TO 8   PREPARATION TIME: 25 MINUTES   COOKING TIME: 1 HOUR

3⅓ cups ricotta cheese
¾ cup plus 1 tablespoon finely grated
　Parmesan cheese
3 extra-large eggs, separated
1 handful basil, leaves torn, plus whole
　leaves for sprinkling
1 handful oregano, leaves roughly
　chopped
2 tablespoons snipped chives
1 teaspoon sea salt
freshly ground black pepper
crisp green salad, to serve

ROASTED TOMATO PESTO:
6 large vine-ripened tomatoes, quartered
　and seeded
⅓ cup extra virgin olive oil, plus extra
　for greasing
½ cup roughly chopped, drained
　sun-dried tomatoes in oil
1 garlic clove, crushed
4 tablespoons blanched almonds, toasted
　and roughly chopped
freshly ground black pepper

Heat the oven to 350°F and lightly grease a deep 8-inch loose-bottomed cake pan.

Put the ricotta, Parmesan and egg yolks in a food processor and blend until smooth and creamy. Transfer the ricotta mixture to a large mixing bowl and stir in the basil, oregano, chives and salt, then season with plenty of freshly ground pepper.

Beat the egg whites in a separate bowl until they will form stiff peaks. Using a large metal spoon, gently fold the whites into the ricotta mixture until combined. Spoon the batter into the prepared pan and smooth the top. Set the pan on a cookie sheet and bake for about 1 hour until risen, set and light golden.

About 30 minutes after you put the cheesecake in the oven, start the roasted tomato pesto. Put the quartered tomatoes in a roasting pan with 2 tablespoons of the oil and season to taste, then turn the tomatoes in the oil. Put them in the oven with the cheesecake and roast for 30 minutes, or until soft and slightly wrinkly.

Remove the tomatoes and cheesecake from the oven and leave the cheesecake to cool slightly while you make the pesto. Put the roasted tomatoes, sun-dried tomatoes, garlic, 2 tablespoons of the nuts and the remaining oil in a food processor and process to a coarse paste; season to taste with salt and pepper. Spoon the pesto into a bowl and add a splash more oil if it seems too dry.

Run a knife around the edge of the cheesecake and remove it from the pan. Scatter the basil leaves and remaining chopped nuts over the top, then serve cut into wedges, with the tomato pesto and a salad.

MUSHROOM, CAMEMBERT & MEMBRILLO WELLINGTONS

The intensely fruity, ruby-red membrillo, or Spanish quince paste or "cheese," is perfect combined with melting Camembert in these individual baked phyllo pastry bundles. Use a Camembert that is just ripe so that it melts but doesn't run away during baking.

SERVES 4   PREPARATION TIME: 15 MINUTES   COOKING TIME: 35 MINUTES

olive oil, for greasing and brushing

4 large portobello mushrooms, about 9 ounces total weight

2 Camembert cheeses, about 5 ounces each

4 tablespoons membrillo

6 sheets phyllo pastry dough, each about 19 x 10 inches

3 tablespoons butter, melted

sea salt and freshly ground black pepper

new potatoes and green salad, to serve

Heat the oven to 375°F and lightly grease a large baking sheet. Brush both sides of each mushroom with olive oil and put them cap-side down on a plate. Season to taste with salt and pepper. Using a sharp knife, slice the rind off the top and bottom of each Camembert; you can leave the rind around the sides. Cut each cheese in half horizontally so you have four equal pieces of cheese.

Put a piece of Camembert on top of each mushroom and top with a tablespoonful of the membrillo.

Cut each sheet of phyllo pastry dough across in half. Layer 3 pieces of phyllo dough, brushing each layer with a little melted butter. Keep the remaining dough covered with a damp dish towel to prevent it from drying out. Sit a stuffed mushroom in the middle of the phyllo stack and draw up the corners of the dough to meet in the middle and make a bundle. Twist the top of the phyllo to seal and brush the bundle with more butter. Repeat with the remaining stuffed mushrooms and dough.

Place the mushroom bundles on the prepared baking sheet. Bake for 25 to 35 minutes until the pastry is golden and crisp. Leave to cool slightly to let the Camembert firm up before serving with boiled new potatoes and a salad.

Membrillo

Membrillo has the texture of a firm fruit jelly with a slight graininess and a sweet, floral taste. Traditionally served with Manchego cheese, it is also delicious cut into cubes and offered with other cheeses. It can also be melted and used as a glaze or in gravies, and works especially well with fatty meats, such as pork or lamb. Although membrillo is the Spanish word for quince, very similar products are made in other countries, such as traditional American fruit cheeses.

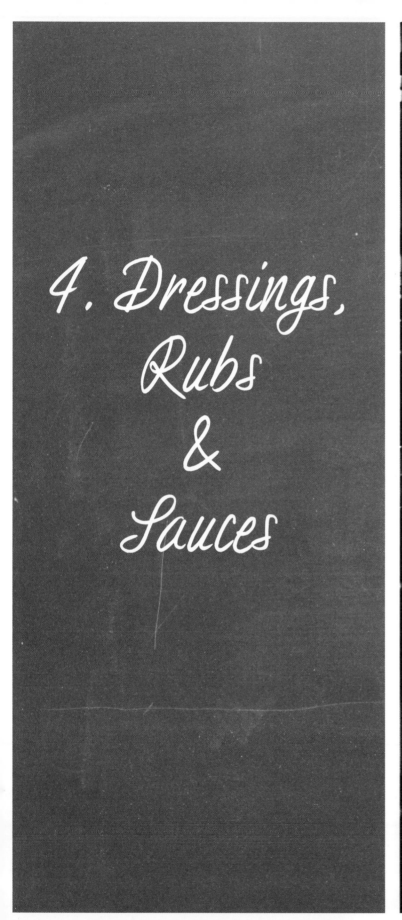

4. Dressings, Rubs & Sauces

DUCK & MANGO SALAD WITH CITRUS DRESSING

Duck and orange are natural partners, with the sour-sweet of the citrus dressing cutting through the rich fattiness of the poultry. This substantial meat salad looks stunning and has just the right balance of flavors and textures.

SERVES 4   PREPARATION TIME: 15 MINUTES   COOKING TIME: 18 MINUTES

4 duck breast halves, skin on,
    about 6 ounces each
4 handfuls baby spinach leaves
1 red onion, thinly sliced
1 small mango, peeled and thinly sliced
1 bunch radishes, sliced
1 cup drained and rinsed canned
    cannellini beans
1 handful cilantro leaves, torn

CITRUS DRESSING:
3 tablespoons extra virgin olive oil
1 teaspoon balsamic vinegar
juice of ½ large orange
½ orange, peeled and flesh chopped
1 red chili, seeded and finely chopped
sea salt and freshly ground black pepper

Heat the oven to 400°F and put a large baking sheet inside to heat.

Put the duck, skin-side down, in a large, dry nonstick skillet. Cook over medium heat for 10 minutes, or until the fat begins to run and the skin is golden brown and crisp. Transfer the duck to the hot baking sheet, skin-side up, and roast for 8 minutes, or until cooked through but slightly pink in the middle. Leave to rest, covered with foil, for 5 minutes.

Meanwhile, put the spinach leaves on a large serving plate. Sprinkle the red onion, mango, radishes and cannellini beans over.

To make the dressing, beat together the olive oil, vinegar and orange juice in a bowl until combined. Stir in the orange flesh and chili and season to taste with salt and pepper.

Cut the duck breasts into slices on the diagonal and put on top of the salad. Spoon the dressing over, then sprinkle with the cilantro. Serve while the duck is still warm.

SALAD OF SMOKED VENISON, ARTICHOKES & QUAIL EGGS WITH WALNUT OIL DRESSING

A sophisticated, impressive salad that is full of flavor: the walnut oil lends a nutty earthiness to the dressing, which complements the richness of the smoked venison.

SERVES 4   PREPARATION TIME: 10 MINUTES   COOKING TIME: 3 MINUTES

12 quail eggs
8 ounces mixed salad leaves, including
   red lettuce
4 or 5 artichoke hearts in oil, drained and
   halved or quartered if large
5 ounces sliced cooked smoked venison,
   or smoked ham, cut into strips
walnut bread slices, to serve

WALNUT OIL DRESSING:
5 tablespoons walnut oil
1 tablespoon extra virgin olive oil
2 tablespoons lemon juice
sea salt and freshly ground black pepper

Mix together the ingredients for the dressing until combined, seasoning to taste with salt and pepper. Leave to one side.

Put the quail eggs in a saucepan, cover with just-boiled water and return to a gentle boil for 2½ minutes. Drain the eggs and cool under cold running water, then peel. Halve the eggs and leave to one side.

Divide the salad leaves among four plates. Top with the artichoke hearts, venison and quail eggs and spoon enough of the dressing over to coat (you will have some dressing left over). Toss lightly before serving immediately with walnut bread.

Smoky Red-Pepper Ketchup

Broiling the bell peppers gives them a delicious smokiness that adds an extra dimension to this ketchup. If making your own ketchup sounds like too much effort, don't worry, because this really is worth the time spent. Everyone will love it—it makes a nice change from the tomato variety.

MAKES ABOUT 2 X 1¼-CUP JARS   PREPARATION TIME: 25 MINUTES
COOKING TIME: 1½ HOURS

6 red bell peppers
2 onions, chopped
2 apples, peeled, cored and chopped
2 celery sticks, sliced
7 tablespoons apple cider vinegar
4 thyme sprigs, leaves removed
½ cup light brown sugar
4 cloves
2 teaspoons ground allspice
½ teaspoon ground cinnamon
½ teaspoon sea salt
few drops hot-pepper sauce, to taste (optional)
freshly ground black pepper

Heat the broiler. Broil the peppers, turning them occasionally, for 30 minutes, or until softened and charred in places. Put the peppers in two plastic bags and leave for 5 minutes, which will make the skins easier to remove. Working over a plate to capture any juices, peel and seed the peppers, then roughly chop the flesh. Strain any juices into a large, nonreactive saucepan.

Process the onions, apples and celery in a food processor until finely chopped, then tip them into the pan. Process the peppers to a coarse puree and add them to the pan with 2 tablespoons of the vinegar, 7 tablespoons water and the thyme leaves.

Bring to a boil, then turn down the heat to low, cover and simmer for 30 minutes, or until the fruit and vegetables are soft. Working in batches, use a food mill or strainer to puree.

Return the puree to the washed and dried pan and add the remaining vinegar, the sugar, cloves, allspice, cinnamon and salt. Season to taste with pepper and bring to a boil, then turn down the heat to low and simmer for 25 to 30 minutes longer until reduced and thickened to a ketchup consistency. Stir regularly to prevent the ketchup from catching on the bottom of the pan. Add a few drops of hot-pepper sauce, if you like a little heat.

Pour into sterilized jars or bottles and seal. The ketchup is ready to use immediately, but will keep for up to 2 months, unopened, in a cool, dark place. Keep refrigerated after opening.

SMOKY RED-PEPPER PORK & ZUCCHINI TZATZIKI

A few spoonfuls of Smoky Red-Pepper Ketchup gives great depth of flavor to this barbecue sauce. A great favorite with kids—something to do with its sweet stickiness no doubt—the sauce is so easy to make. All you need is a handful of everyday staple ingredients to make this condiment-cum-marinade.

SERVES 4   PREPARATION TIME: 20 MINUTES, PLUS MARINATING
COOKING TIME: 8 MINUTES

4 pork steaks or blade steaks, about
    6 ounces each, fat trimmed
4 Mediterranean or Middle Eastern
    flatbreads, warmed
½ cup drained and sliced roasted or
    grilled red bell peppers (from a jar)
1 red chili, seeded and thinly sliced
2 tablespoons roughly chopped
    cilantro leaves

BARBECUE SAUCE:
4 tablespoons Smoky Red-Pepper
    Ketchup (see facing page) or
    regular ketchup

2 tablespoons balsamic vinegar
2 tablespoons honey
1 tablespoon dark soy sauce
2 teaspoons olive oil

ZUCCHINI TZATZIKI:
⅔ cup plain yogurt
4 tablespoons lemon juice
1 garlic clove, crushed
1 zucchini, coarsely grated
sea salt and freshly ground black pepper

Mix together all the ingredients for the barbecue sauce. Put the pork in a nonmetallic dish and spoon the barbecue sauce over, turning to coat both sides of the meat. Leave to marinate, covered, for 1 hour in the refrigerator.

Heat the broiler and line the broiler pan with foil. Broil the pork for 4 minutes on each side, or until cooked to your liking. (If you have a combined broiler/oven, you can warm the flatbreads at the same time and then wrap them in foil to keep them warm.) Cover the pork with foil and leave to rest for 5 minutes.

Meanwhile, mix together the ingredients for the zucchini tzatziki, seasoning to taste with salt and pepper. Leave to one side.

To serve, slice the pork into strips and arrange on the warmed flatbreads. Pour over any juices left in the foil after resting, then top with the red peppers, the tzatziki, chili and cilantro.

Thai Lemongrass & Chili Oil

Flavored oils are a real asset to your pantry, and are a simple way of adding an instant burst of flavor with very little effort. Herbs and spices are the most obvious flavorings, but you can also add garlic, dried mushrooms, lemon zest or shallots, among many other ingredients. If you have an abundance of fresh herbs, one of the simplest ways to preserve them is in oil (or vinegar). Flavored oils are best made in relatively small quantities, because they contain fresh ingredients and will deteriorate with time. I think organic flavorings are best. Make sure they are completely dry before adding them to the oil. This flavored oil captures many of the flavors of Thai cooking—just add a splash to dressings, Asian soups, curries and noodle and rice dishes.

MAKES ABOUT 1½ CUPS   PREPARATION TIME: 10 MINUTES, PLUS COOLING AND 3 DAYS INFUSING   COOKING TIME: 5 MINUTES

1½ cups light or mild olive oil, plus extra if needed
½ teaspoon dried chili flakes
2 red chilies, halved or quartered
2 lemongrass stalks, outer layers removed and the stalks bruised
4 kaffir lime leaves
1 teaspoon sea salt
2 long Thai basil sprigs

Pour the olive oil into a small saucepan and add the chili flakes, chilies, lemongrass and lime leaves. Heat the oil for 3 minutes over medium-low heat. Heating the oil encourages the flavors to infuse efficiently and quickly. Stir in the salt (this will help to keep the oil clear) and leave the oil to cool.

Insert the basil sprigs into a 1-pint sterilized bottle. Using tongs, transfer the lemongrass, fresh chilies and lime leaves from the oil to the bottle. Using a funnel, pour the oil and chili flakes into the bottle until the other ingredients are submerged. It is important that the oil covers the flavorings—if it doesn't, add a little extra oil.

Put the lid on and leave the oil and flavorings to infuse for 3 days in the refrigerator, turning the bottle occasionally. Store in the refrigerator and use within 2 weeks.

BEEF CARPACCIO SALAD WITH **THAI LEMONGRASS & CHILI OIL** DRESSING

Sweet, sour, salty and hot—this fragrant Thai dressing ticks all the right boxes, and rather than masking the earthy flavors of the raw beef, it lifts and complements them. Note that the recipe specifies to put the beef in the freezer first for 30 minutes, because this makes it so much easier to slice thinly. Another useful tip is to use a very sharp, long, thin knife for slicing. Choose a thick piece of beef, preferably a middle cut, so you can cut descent-size slices.

SERVES 4   PREPARATION TIME: 15 MINUTES, PLUS FREEZING

7 ounces good-quality boneless sirloin steak, in one piece
2 handfuls baby spinach leaves
1 carrot, thinly sliced into thin strips
2-inch piece English cucumber, quartered lengthwise, seeded and cut into thin strips
1 small red bell pepper, seeded and cut into thin strips
¼ small red onion, very thinly sliced
1 small handful basil, leaves roughly torn
1 small handful cilantro, leaves roughly chopped

DRESSING:
3 tablespoons Thai Lemongrass & Chili Oil (see facing page)
2 tablespoons fish sauce
juice of 1 lime
1 teaspoon sugar
sea salt and freshly ground black pepper

Put the steak in the freezer for 30 minutes to firm it up and make it easier to slice.

Meanwhile, mix together all the ingredients for the dressing, seasoning to taste with salt and pepper. Leave to one side.

Divide the spinach among four plates and top with the carrot, cucumber and red pepper. Spoon enough of the dressing over to coat and toss lightly until combined.

Remove the steak from the freezer and, using a very sharp, long knife, cut into very thin, elegant slices. As you cut, put the slices on a plate and keep covered with plastic wrap to prevent them from discoloring while you slice the remaining steak. If you put a layer of plastic wrap between the layers, you'll be able to separate the slices more easily.

Arrange the steak on each serving of salad, season to taste with salt and pepper and scatter the red onion and herbs over the top. Spoon more of the dressing over, to taste, and serve immediately.

SHRIMP FRITTERS WITH SWEET CHILI JAM

A great combination of sweet and sticky, this fiery chili jam can be served as a dip, stirred into oriental sauces or turned into a marinade for meat, poultry and seafood. It's also perfect with these Asian fritters.

SERVES 4 (CHILI JAM MAKES 2 X 7-OUNCE JARS)   PREPARATION TIME: 30 MINUTES
COOKING TIME: 35 MINUTES

12 ounces raw large, shelled shrimp
2 zucchini, coarsely grated
1 red chili, seeded and finely chopped
5 tablespoons all-purpose flour, plus extra
  for dusting
1 teaspoon baking powder
2 teaspoons ground coriander
½ teaspoon turmeric
2 scallions, finely chopped
2 tablespoons chopped cilantro leaves
1 teaspoon salt
2 eggs, beaten
peanut oil, for frying
freshly ground black pepper

shredded heart of lettuce, shredded
  scallions and lime wedges, to serve

SWEET CHILI JAM:
1½-inch piece fresh gingerroot,
  peeled and finely chopped
3 garlic cloves, peeled
2 red chilies, halved
2 tablespoons Thai fish sauce
2¼ cups peeled, seeded and
  chopped tomatoes
1 cup sugar
5 tablespoons rice wine vinegar
  or white wine vinegar

To make the sweet chili jam, put the ginger, garlic, chilies and fish sauce into a food processor or blender and whiz to a puree. Put the puree in a saucepan with the tomatoes, sugar and vinegar and bring to a boil. Turn down the heat to low and simmer for 15 to 25 minutes, stirring regularly, until thick with a jamlike consistency. Pour into sterilized jars, cover with lids and leave to cool, or pour straight into a serving bowl to cool.

To make the fritters, reserve 12 shrimp and finely chop the remainder. Put the chopped shrimp, zucchini, chili, flour, baking powder, spices, scallions, cilantro, salt and eggs into a mixing bowl. Season to taste with pepper and stir until combined into a thick batter.

Heat about 1½ inches oil in a large wok or large, deep skillet until very hot.

Take a small spoonful of the shrimp mixture in your floured hand, form into a patty and press a whole shrimp into the middle. Shape 3 more small patties in the same way. (The patties will be very soft but will firm up when cooked.) Lower them into the hot oil and fry for 2 to 3 minutes, occasionally spooning the hot oil over them, until the shrimp are pink and the fritters are golden brown all over. Drain on paper towels and keep warm in a low oven while you shape and fry the remaining fritters—you should have 12 in total.

Serve the fritters hot, with the sweet chili jam, shredded lettuce and scallions, and lime wedges for squeezing over.

HALLOUMI, CHICKPEA & RED ONION SALAD WITH POMEGRANATE MOLASSES DRESSING

The pomegranate molasses dressing here has a delicious sweet, tangy flavor, perfect for this chunky Middle Eastern-style salad. It is best served when the halloumi is still warm, with pita bread or flatbreads.

SERVES 4   PREPARATION TIME: 15 MINUTES   COOKING TIME: 4 MINUTES

1 head romaine, roughly chopped
2 cans (15-oz.) chickpeas, drained and rinsed
1 small red onion, sliced
1 small English cucumber, seeded and diced
10 ounces halloumi cheese, patted dry and cut into 8 slices
olive oil, for brushing
1 small pomegranate, cut in half and seeds removed

2 tablespoons chopped mint leaves
2 tablespoons chopped cilantro leaves

POMEGRANATE MOLASSES DRESSING:
4 tablespoons extra virgin olive oil
2 tablespoons pomegranate molasses or pomegranate syrup
1 teaspoon lemon juice
½ teaspoon sugar
sea salt and freshly ground black pepper

Mix together the ingredients for the dressing in a nonmetallic bowl, seasoning to taste with salt and pepper. Leave to one side until ready to use.

Divide the lettuce, chickpeas, red onion and cucumber onto four serving plates. Spoon the dressing over and lightly toss until everything is mixed together.

Heat a large cast-iron, ridged grill pan over high heat. Brush the halloumi with a little oil. Reduce the heat a little and grill the halloumi for about 2 minutes on each side, or until soft and golden brown in places.

Set the warm halloumi on the salad and scatter the pomegranate seeds, mint and cilantro over the top.

Pomegranate Molasses

A key ingredient in Middle Eastern cooking, pomegranate molasses is a tangy reduction of pomegranate juice, sugar and lemon juice. Its sweet-sour flavor and thick, sticky consistency make it a useful addition to marinades, glazes and dressings, and it goes particularly well with poultry, pork, lamb and vegetables.

CHARGRILLED EGGPLANT & SKORTHALIA ON CROSTINI

This is definitely one for garlic lovers! Skorthalia is a rich and creamy Greek sauce-cum-dip made with bread, ground pistachios, lemon juice and more than a hint of garlic. You can scatter pomegranate seeds over the crostini instead of the parsley, if preferred.

MAKES 8   PREPARATION TIME: 20 MINUTES, PLUS COOLING   COOKING TIME: 5 MINUTES

8 large, thick baguette slices
7 ounces chargrilled or roasted eggplants
   in oil (from a jar), drained and sliced
   if necessary
2 tablespoons chopped flat-leaf parsley
   leaves
tossed green salad, to serve

SKORTHALIA:
4 slices day-old white bread, crusts
   removed and torn into pieces
⅓ cup unsalted shelled pistachios
2 garlic cloves
juice of ½ lemon
3 to 4 tablespoons extra virgin olive oil
sea salt and freshly ground black pepper

To make the skorthalia, soak the bread in 1 cup water. Finely chop the pistachios in a food processor, then add the soaked bread, garlic and lemon juice. Blend to a smooth, creamy consistency. Gradually pour in the olive oil, blending until the skorthalia is as thick as mayonnaise. Season to taste with salt and pepper.

Heat the broiler. Toast the baguette slices under the broiler until golden brown on both sides, then leave to cool. Top each with a slice of eggplant and a generous spoonful of skorthalia (keep any leftover skorthalia, covered with plastic wrap, in the refrigerator). Scatter the parsley over and serve with a tossed salad.

LEBANESE CHICKEN WITH SPICED LEMON OIL

This chicken comes with fattoush, a Lebanese salad made from vibrant, crunchy vegetables and pieces of crisp, toasted pita bread. Here it's dressed in a lightly spiced, aromatic lemon oil.

SERVES 4 (SPICED LEMON OIL MAKES A 7-OUNCE BOTTLE)
PREPARATION TIME: 30 MINUTES, PLUS 8 HOURS INFUSING   COOKING TIME: 30 MINUTES

3 tablespoons za'atar spice mix
8 chicken thighs, each slashed 3 times
sea salt and freshly ground black pepper

SPICED LEMON OIL:
¾ cup plus 2 tablespoons extra virgin
   olive oil
3 strips pared lemon zest
1 unwaxed lemon, quartered
2 garlic cloves, peeled
2 teaspoons coriander seeds
1 teaspoon black peppercorns
1 star anise
2 bay leaves
½ teaspoon coarse sea salt

FATTOUSH:
1 pita bread
1½ cups vine-ripened cherry tomatoes,
   halved
1 small English cucumber, quartered
   lengthwise, seeded and cut into
   bite-size pieces
1 red bell pepper, seeded and cut
   into bite-size pieces
5 radishes, sliced
4 tablespoons chopped mint leaves
4 tablespoons chopped flat-leaf parsley
   leaves
½ teaspoon cumin seeds, toasted

To make the lemon oil, put all the ingredients into a saucepan and warm for a few minutes. Remove from the heat, cover and leave to infuse for 8 hours in a cool place. Remove the garlic and lemon zest. Squeeze the juice from the lemon into the oil and discard the quarters. Decant the oil into a sterilized bottle and seal. It is ready to be used now, but its flavor will intensify after a few days. Keep in the refrigerator for up to 2 weeks.

Heat the oven to 375°F. Rub the za'atar over each chicken thigh and season to taste with salt and pepper. Put the thighs in a roasting pan and roast for 20 to 25 minutes until cooked through.

Meanwhile, make the fattoush. Toast both sides of the pita bread in a large, heavy-bottomed skillet until starting to crisp. Remove from the pan and split open, then toast the inside of the pita until crisp. Leave to cool, then break the pita into large, bite-size pieces. Put the tomatoes, cucumber, red pepper, radishes and herbs in a serving bowl. Spoon 3 tablespoons of the spiced lemon oil over the top and toss until combined. Sprinkle with the cumin seeds. Before serving, toss the pita into the salad and serve with the chicken thighs.

Za'atar Spice Mix

Za'atar is a versatile Middle Eastern spice mix, made from ground sumac berries, sesame seeds and herbs in varying proportions. You can buy it, although it's easy to make your own.

PAN-GRILLED CHICKEN ON POLENTA WITH SUMMER HERB PESTO

There are many variations on classic pesto, the basil sauce from around Genoa, in Italy. Okay, they might not all be authentic, but many are no less delicious, especially if they are homemade. In this version, basil is joined by fresh thyme, oregano and chives, and the pine nuts are replaced by pistachios. If you have any pesto left over, store it in a covered container in the refrigerator, making sure there is a layer of olive oil covering the pesto to keep it fresh.

SERVES 4   PREPARATION TIME: 30 MINUTES, PLUS MARINATING
COOKING TIME: 30 MINUTES

4 boneless, skinless chicken breast
  halves, about 6 ounces each
6½ cups good-quality chicken stock
1¼ cups polenta
Parmesan cheese shavings,
  to serve (optional)

MARINADE:
2 tablespoons olive oil
1 large garlic clove, sliced
1 tablespoon balsamic vinegar
6 long thyme sprigs, leaves removed

SUMMER HERB PESTO:
1¼ cups basil leaves
1 ounce oregano sprigs, leaves removed
4 long thyme sprigs, leaves removed
¼ cup unsalted shelled pistachios
½ cup extra virgin olive oil
1 clove garlic, crushed
2 tablespoons snipped chives
1 tablespoon finely grated Parmesan
  cheese
sea salt and freshly ground black pepper

Put the chicken breasts between two large sheets of plastic wrap and flatten slightly with a meat mallet or the end of a rolling pin; you want the breasts to have an even thickness. Mix together all the ingredients for the marinade in a large, nonmetallic dish. Season to taste with salt and pepper, then add the chicken. Turn the chicken until it is coated and leave to marinate, covered, for about 1 hour in the refrigerator.

To make the pesto, put the basil, oregano, thyme and pistachios in a mini food processor and process until finely chopped. With the motor running, gradually add the oil and blend until it makes a coarse puree. Spoon the pesto into a bowl and stir in the garlic, chives and Parmesan. Season to taste with salt and pepper. Leave to one side until ready to use.

To cook the polenta, bring the stock to a boil in a large, heavy-bottomed saucepan and rain in the polenta in a steady stream, stirring. Turn down the heat and simmer, stirring regularly, for 25 to 30 minutes, until the polenta is smooth and creamy and starting to come away from the side of the pan.

Meanwhile, heat a cast-iron, ridged grill pan and grill the chicken in two batches for about 5 minutes on each side until cooked through. Remove the chicken from the pan as each batch is cooked and cover with foil. Leave the chicken to rest for 10 minutes while the polenta finishes cooking. Put the polenta on four plates and top with the chicken. Spoon a little of the pan juices over and serve each portion with a large spoonful of pesto. Add a small amount of shaved Parmesan, if you like.

GLAZED PORK TENDERLOIN IN CHINESE PLUM SAUCE

Similar in taste and consistency to the classic hoisin sauce, this star anise-infused plum sauce makes a sticky, golden glaze for the pork, but it is equally as good used in stir-fries or Asian noodle and rice dishes. It will keep for six months stored in a cool, dark place and one month after opening (keep in the refrigerator).

SERVES 4 (CHINESE PLUM SAUCE MAKES 2 X 1¾-CUP JARS)
PREPARATION TIME: 30 MINUTES, PLUS MARINATING   COOKING TIME: 1½ HOURS

1½ pounds pork tenderloin, trimmed
   of any fat and silverskin
sea salt and freshly ground black pepper
steamed Thai jasmine rice and bok choy,
   to serve
sesame seeds, to serve

CHINESE PLUM SAUCE:
1 onion, chopped
5 large garlic cloves, chopped

1 Thai chili, chopped
3-inch piece fresh gingerroot, peeled and
   grated
2¾ cups pitted and chopped dark plums
2 tablespoons dark soy sauce
⅔ cup rice vinegar
2 star anise, very finely ground
1 cup plus 2 tablespoons sugar
1 tablespoon honey

To make the Chinese plum sauce, put the onion, garlic, chili, ginger, plums, soy sauce, vinegar and star anise in a nonreactive pan. Bring to a boil, then turn down the heat to low and simmer, stirring occasionally, for 25 minutes, or until the plums break down into a pulp.

Pass the plum mixture through a strainer to make a coarse puree; discard the solids that are left. Return the puree to the pan and stir in the sugar and honey. Bring to a boil, then turn down the heat and simmer for 20 to 30 minutes until reduced and with a saucelike consistency. Spoon into sterilized jars and cover. Alternatively, use a portion of the sauce right away and pack the rest in a sterilized jar.

Spoon 6 tablespoons of the plum sauce over the pork and leave to marinate, covered, for at least 30 minutes.

Heat the oven to 350°F. Put the sauce-covered pork on a piece of foil large enough to enclose it, then season to taste with salt and pepper. Bring together the sides of the foil, scrunch the top to make a loose package and put it on a baking sheet. Bake for 20 minutes, then transfer the package to a plate.

Heat the broiler. Open up the foil package and pour the pork juices into a small pan. Spoon another 3 tablespoons of the sauce over the pork and broil for 5 minutes, or until golden brown and glazed. Transfer the pork to a warm plate, cover loosely with foil and leave to rest for 5 minutes.

Meanwhile, pour any juices from the foil package into the small pan and heat through. Serve the pork, sliced on the diagonal, with jasmine rice and bok choy. Spoon the hot juices over the top and sprinkle with sesame seeds.

Garlic & Fennel Mustard

This wholegrain mustard has just the right amount of crunch, along with a hint of garlic and fennel. It's great with the usual suspects, but you can also add it to marinades, sauces and rubs. An immersion blender makes easy work of breaking down the mustard seeds, but you can also use a mini food processor or mortar and pestle.

MAKES 3 X 7-OUNCE JARS   PREPARATION TIME: 20 MINUTES, PLUS 1 MONTH MATURING

⅔ cup yellow mustard seeds
2 tablespoons brown mustard seeds
2 teaspoons fennel seeds
¼ teaspoon turmeric
2 teaspoons salt
¼ teaspoon ground black pepper
1¼ cups apple cider vinegar
½ cup packed light brown sugar
1 large garlic clove, crushed

Put both mustard seeds, the fennel seeds, turmeric, salt and pepper in a tall, narrow beaker or jug. Add half the vinegar and leave for 5 minutes to soften, then blend the mixture using an immersion blender. Blend well, making sure you break up most of the seeds, until the mixture starts to become thick.

Add the remaining vinegar, sugar and garlic and continue to blend until thick. Check the seasoning, then pack into sterilized jars. Seal and store in a cool, dark, dry place for up to 6 months. The flavor will mellow with time and will be ready to eat in about 1 month.

GARLIC & FENNEL MUSTARD-CRUSTED
LEG OF LAMB & POT-ROASTED PEARS

The wholegrain mustard not only creates a flavorsome crust when roasted, but also helps to keep the lamb moist and succulent. Serve the lamb in thick slices with the sweet, golden baked pears and any favorite roast meat accompaniments.

**SERVES 4   PREPARATION TIME: 15 MINUTES, PLUS MARINATING AND RESTING
COOKING TIME: 1 HOUR 5 MINUTES**

6 tablespoons Garlic & Fennel Mustard
   (see facing page)
2 tablespoons finely chopped rosemary
2 tablespoons olive oil
1 half leg of lamb roast, bone in, about
   2¾ pounds

2 garlic cloves, cut into matchsticks
2 tablespoons balsamic vinegar
4 pears, peeled and halved lengthwise
sea salt and freshly ground black pepper

Mix together the mustard, rosemary and half of the olive oil. Using a sharp knife or skewer, make small, deep cuts into the lamb. Insert the matchsticks of garlic into the cuts, pressing them into the lamb, then spread the mustard mixture over in a thick layer. Put the lamb in a roasting pan and leave to marinate, covered, for 1 hour at room temperature. Season generously with salt and pepper.

Heat the oven to 425°F. Put a splash of water in the bottom of the roasting pan and roast the lamb for 20 minutes. Reduce the oven temperature to 350°F and roast the lamb for 10 minutes longer, then remove from the oven.

Mix together the remaining olive oil and the balsamic vinegar. Brush the mixture over the pears and put them around the lamb in the roasting pan. Return to the oven and roast, occasionally basting the lamb with the juices in the pan, for 30 to 35 minutes until the meat is cooked, but still pink in the middle, and the pears are tender.

Cover the pan with foil and leave the lamb to rest for 15 minutes. (You can use the juices in the pan to make a gravy.) Carve the lamb into thick slices and serve with the pears.

TAGLIATA WITH CHIMICHURRI SAUCE

This is a twist on the Italian tagliata, the classic seared steak, arugula and Parmesan salad. Instead of the usual splash of balsamic vinegar to finish the dish, it comes with a new take on chimichurri, which can loosely be described as Argentinian pesto sauce.

SERVES 4   PREPARATION TIME: 20 MINUTES   COOKING TIME: 6 MINUTES

2 steaks, such as boneless rib-eye or sirloin, each about 9 ounces and ¾-inch thick, at room temperature
1 tablespoon olive oil
3 ounces arugula leaves
2 large vine-ripened tomatoes, quartered, seeded and diced
2 ounces Parmesan cheese, shaved into thin slices
sea salt and freshly ground black pepper
ciabatta bread, to serve

CHIMICHURRI SAUCE:
1 large handful basil leaves, chopped
1 tablespoon chopped oregano leaves
4 tablespoons chopped parsley leaves
2 garlic cloves, crushed
½ cup olive oil
3 tablespoons sherry vinegar or red wine vinegar
1 teaspoon ground coriander
½ teaspoon dried chili flakes
½ teaspoon salt

To make the chimichurri sauce, mix together all the ingredients in a bowl, seasoning to taste with salt and pepper, then leave to one side.

Brush the steaks with the olive oil and season to taste with salt and pepper.

Heat a large cast-iron, ridged grill pan over high heat. Sear the steaks for 2 to 3 minutes on each side, turning once or twice. Remove them from the pan and leave to rest, covered with foil, for 5 minutes.

Meanwhile, make the salad. Scatter the arugula and tomatoes over four serving plates. Cut the steak into ½-inch slices and put on top of the salad. Spoon as much of the chimichurri sauce over as you like and sprinkle with the Parmesan before serving with slices of ciabatta.

Chimichurri

Chimichurri is one of the most versatile sauces. In Argentina, it is traditionally served with grilled steak, but it also works well with lamb, chicken, vegetables and seafood. Use as a sauce, marinade, dip or salad dressing, or stir into pasta like pesto sauce. Feel free to alter the proportions of the herbs, spices and garlic, as preferred, or even add chopped tomatoes, roasted red bell peppers or finely chopped toasted nuts.

Mayonnaise

I learned to make mayonnaise as a child from my mother and I've been making the same recipe ever since, although I've sometimes added the odd twist over the years. Homemade mayonnaise bears little resemblance to the commercial versions, and it's really satisfying to make. You need to add the oil very slowly in a steady stream to avoid the mixture separating. You can beat the mayonnaise by hand, but an immersion blender is very effective. I recommend a light, neutral oil, such as sunflower, because a strong-flavored one, such as olive oil, can be overpowering. Great on its own, mayonnaise also makes a superb foundation for other sauces and dips: try adding Sweet Chili Jam (see page 112), herbs, garlic, anchovies, lemon juice or creamed horseradish—there's a multitude of options.

MAKES 2 X 9-OUNCE JARS   PREPARATION TIME: 10 MINUTES

1 egg
2 tablespoons white wine vinegar
2 tablespoons Dijon mustard
2 teaspoons sugar
a pinch each sea salt and freshly ground black pepper
1¾ cups vegetable oil

Crack the egg into a tall, narrow beaker or jug. Add the vinegar, mustard, sugar, salt and pepper and blend using an immersion blender until combined.

Very slowly add the vegetable oil in a steady stream, blending continuously, until the mixture becomes opaque and thickens to a smooth, glossy sauce. Be careful not to add too much oil initially, or the mixture might separate. If it does separate, you can reclaim it by gradually adding the separated mixture to a second egg-and-mustard base and starting again.

Check the seasoning and spoon into two sterilized jars, then cover with lids. Store in the refrigerator for up to 4 weeks.

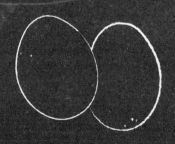

CRAB & SHRIMP CAKES WITH SWEET CHILI **MAYONNAISE**

These are truly gourmet fish cakes! Use fresh crabmeat and freshly cooked shrimp for the best flavor and texture. The cakes can be made up to a day in advance and stored in the refrigerator until ready to cook. If you don't have time to make your own mayonnaise, a good-quality store-bought version is nearly as good.

SERVES 4   PREPARATION TIME: 30 MINUTES   COOKING TIME: 35 MINUTES

1½ pounds Idaho or other baking
   potatoes, peeled and halved
2 large garlic cloves, cut in half
9 ounces cooked shelled shrimp,
   roughly chopped
14 ounces white crabmeat
2 tablespoons chopped parsley leaves
2 scallions, green part only, finely
   chopped
finely grated zest of 1 small lemon
all-purpose flour, for dusting

6 tablespoons vegetable oil
sea salt and freshly ground black pepper
crisp green salad and lemon wedges,
   to serve

SWEET CHILI MAYONNAISE:
½ cup Mayonnaise (see facing page)
2 tablespoons Sweet Chili Jam
   (see page 112) or sweet chili sauce
juice of 1 lime

To make the sweet chili mayonnaise, stir the mayonnaise with the sweet chili jam, lime juice and 1 to 2 tablespoons warm water until combined to a saucelike consistency. Leave to one side.

Cook the potatoes and garlic in a pan of boiling salted water for 15 to 20 minutes until tender. Drain the potatoes and garlic in a colander, then return them to the pan to dry in the heat of the pan. Leave to cool slightly, then lift out the garlic and mash until smooth in a large bowl. Coarsely grate the potatoes into the bowl and season with plenty of salt and pepper.

Add the shrimp, crabmeat, parsley, scallions and lemon zest to the bowl and stir until combined.

Make a layer of flour on a plate and flour your hands. Divide the potato mixture into 8 portions and form each into a round cake about ¾ inch thick. Lightly coat each cake in flour and set on a clean plate. You can either chill the seafood cakes at this stage or cook them right away. Heat the oven to 100°F.

Heat half the vegetable oil in a large, nonstick skillet over medium heat. Fry the seafood cakes, in two batches, for about 4 minutes on each side until golden brown and crisp. Drain the seafood cakes on paper towels and keep them warm in the low oven while you cook the second batch, adding more oil as needed. Serve with the sweet chili mayonnaise, a crisp green salad and lemon wedges.

HARISSA & TOMATO COUSCOUS WITH LEMON-ROASTED VEGETABLES

Fans of harissa, the fiery North African paste, will love this dish, because it not only adds heaps of flavor to the couscous and accompanying mayonnaise, but is also a wonderful warm flavor.

SERVES 4   PREPARATION TIME: 20 MINUTES   COOKING TIME: 40 MINUTES

6 ounces cherry tomatoes on the vine
4 large garlic cloves
1 eggplant, thinly sliced lengthwise
2 zucchini, thinly sliced lengthwise
2 red onions, peeled and cut into wedges
2 romano or other large red bell peppers, seeded and quartered lengthwise
4 tablespoons Spiced Lemon Oil (see page 116)
4 roasted artichokes (from a jar), drained and halved if large

1⅓ cups couscous
1¼ cups good-quality just-boiled chicken stock
2 teaspoons harissa paste
⅔ cup blanched almonds
1 handful basil leaves (optional)
sea salt and freshly ground black pepper

HARISSA MAYONNAISE:
2 teaspoons harissa paste
4 tablespoons good-quality mayonnaise

Heat the oven to 400°F. Divide the tomatoes, garlic, eggplant, zucchini, onions and red peppers between two large roasting pans. Generously brush the vegetables with lemon oil and roast for 20 minutes, or until the tomatoes and garlic are soft. Turn the vegetables, add the artichokes and brush with more lemon oil, then roast for 20 minutes longer, or until the vegetables are tender and charred in places. While the vegetables are roasting, put the couscous in a heatproof bowl, pour the chicken stock over and stir, then cover. Set aside for 5 minutes, or until the couscous absorbs the stock, then fluff up with a fork.

Remove the cherry tomatoes from the vines and peel the roasted garlic. Put the tomatoes and garlic in a mini food processor with 1 tablespoon of the lemon oil and the harissa. Process to make a smooth sauce, then season to taste with salt and pepper and stir into the couscous. Cover with a plate and leave to one side. Toast the almonds in a dry skillet over medium heat for 5 minutes, turning once, or until starting to turn golden. Mix together the ingredients for the harissa mayonnaise with 1 teaspoon warm water. Scatter the almonds over the couscous and serve with the vegetables, harissa mayonnaise and basil leaves.

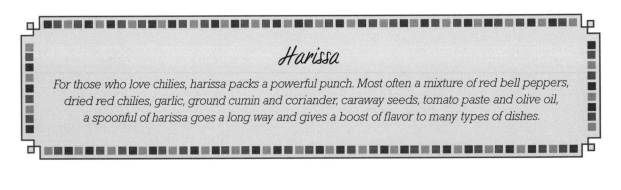

Harissa

For those who love chilies, harissa packs a powerful punch. Most often a mixture of red bell peppers, dried red chilies, garlic, ground cumin and coriander, caraway seeds, tomato paste and olive oil, a spoonful of harissa goes a long way and gives a boost of flavor to many types of dishes.

5. Vegetables

Preserved Mushrooms in Oil

These mushrooms take on a hint of the lemon and herbs, but retain their woody, earthy flavors.
Serve them as part of an antipasti, as a topping for bruschetta or as a simple pasta sauce.

MAKES A 1-QUART JAR   PREPARATION TIME: 10 MINUTES, PLUS 3 DAYS MATURING
COOKING TIME: 13 MINUTES

½ cup apple cider vinegar
3 garlic cloves, halved
6 long thyme sprigs
4 long rosemary sprigs
2 teaspoons coarse sea salt
1 teaspoon black peppercorns
1 pound 10 ounces mixed mushrooms of varying size and type, such as baby button, cremini, enoki,
shiitake, oyster, girolles or chanterelles, any dirt wiped off and the stems trimmed, if necessary
pared zest of ½ unwaxed lemon
2 bay leaves
about 1¾ cups good-quality olive oil, to cover

Combine the vinegar, 2 cups water, the garlic, half the thyme and rosemary, the salt and peppercorns in
a large, nonreactive saucepan. Bring to a boil, then turn down the heat and stir until the salt dissolves.
Add the mushrooms, then simmer for 10 minutes, or until soft and cooked through. Drain well
in a strainer and remove the garlic, thyme and rosemary. Discard the vinegar mixture.

Put the mushrooms, peppercorns, zest, bay leaves and remaining thyme and rosemary in a sterilized jar.
Pour in enough oil to cover the ingredients. Use a plastic skewer to get rid of air pockets, then seal. Store
in a cool, dry, dark place. The mushrooms can be eaten after 3 days and are best eaten within 2 weeks.

POLENTA BRUSCHETTA WITH **PRESERVED MUSHROOMS** & SMOKED DUCK

Slices of crisply broiled polenta make a refreshing bruschetta and provide the perfect base for this mushroom and smoked duck topping. Feel free to replace the duck with an alternative cooked or cured meat or poultry—ham, salami, chorizo or slices of roast chicken, beef or lamb all work well.

SERVES 4   PREPARATION TIME: 10 MINUTES, PLUS SETTING   COOKING TIME: 25 MINUTES

¼ recipe quantity Preserved Mushrooms
  in Oil (see facing page), drained
2 skinless smoked duck breast halves,
  cut into strips
2 tablespoons chopped parsley leaves

POLENTA BRUSCHETTA:
1¼ cups instant polenta
3 tablespoons butter
½ cup finely grated Parmesan cheese
olive oil, for greasing and brushing
sea salt and freshly ground black pepper

To make the polenta bruschetta, put 3⅔ cups water in a saucepan and gradually stir in the polenta, then bring to a boil. Turn down the heat to low and simmer, stirring, for 10 minutes, or until you have a thick, smooth paste that comes away from the side of the pan. Remove the pan from the heat and stir in the butter and Parmesan. Season to taste with salt and pepper.

Lightly grease a baking sheet and spread out the polenta into an even layer, about ¾ inch thick. Smooth the top and leave to cool and set.

Heat the broiler. Cut the polenta into 4 squares, then cut each square into 2 triangles. Brush the polenta with a little olive oil, put on a broiler rack and broil for 12 minutes, turning once, until crisp and golden. Top each polenta triangle with a large spoonful of preserved mushrooms, a few slices of duck and a sprinkling of parsley. Season to taste with salt and pepper and serve warm.

Types of Polenta

Golden yellow polenta makes a great alternative to bread, potatoes, rice or pasta. This cornmeal comes in various forms. Traditional coarsely ground polenta takes a while to cook, but I think it has the best flavor. There's also finely ground, super-quick instant polenta, used here, as well as slabs of polenta you can buy, ready to be sliced and fried, broiled or pan-grilled.

ROASTED RED-PEPPER GAZPACHO WITH SERRANO CHIPS

Choose the most flavorsome, fragrant, vine-ripened tomatoes you can find and you'll be rewarded with the best-tasting gazpacho.

SERVES 4   PREPARATION TIME: 25 MINUTES, PLUS CHILLING   COOKING TIME: 25 MINUTES

2 romano or other large red bell peppers
2¼ pounds large vine-ripened tomatoes
2 slices day-old bread, crusts removed
1 English cucumber, peeled, seeded and chopped
1 green chili, seeded and chopped
1 garlic clove, halved
3 tablespoons extra virgin olive oil
juice of 1 lime and 1 lemon
1 teaspoon sugar

a few drops hot-pepper sauce
4 to 6 slices Serrano ham
small handful basil leaves, for sprinkling
sea salt and freshly ground black pepper

CROUTONS:
2 slices day-old bread, crusts removed
1 garlic clove, halved lengthwise
2 tablespoons olive oil

Heat the broiler. Broil the peppers, turning them occasionally, for 15 minutes, or until they are soft and charred in places. Put the peppers in a plastic bag and leave for 5 minutes, which will make the skins easier to remove. Remove the skin and seeds and discard, and leave the peppers to one side.

Meanwhile, using a small, sharp knife, cut a shallow cross in the bottom of each tomato, then put them in a large heatproof bowl and cover with just-boiled water. Leave the tomatoes to stand for 2 minutes, then drain. Peel off and discard the tomato skins, then seed and cut the flesh into chunks. Leave to one side.

Soak the bread in ⅔ cup water in a shallow dish for 5 minutes, or until it absorbs most of the water. Remove the bread from the dish and tear into chunks.

Put half the bread, peppers, tomatoes, cucumber, chili, garlic, extra virgin olive oil and lime and lemon juices in a blender with ¾ cup plus 2 tablespoons cold water and blend until combined but still chunky. Repeat with the remaining ingredients and another ¾ cup plus 2 tablespoons cold water. Combine the two batches in a large pitcher, stir in the sugar and a few drops of hot pepper sauce and season to taste with salt and pepper. Chill, covered, for 2 to 3 hours.

To make the croutons, rub the bread slices with the cut side of the garlic clove. Cut the bread into cubes and put them in a small plastic bag with the oil. Seal the bag and shake gently to coat the bread in the oil. Heat a large, nonstick skillet over medium heat and fry the croutons for 6 to 8 minutes until crisp and golden brown all over. Leave them to drain on paper towels.

Wipe the skillet clean and add the ham in a single layer. Cook for 3 minutes, turning once, or until crisp. Remove from the pan and leave to cool slightly, then break into large bite-size pieces. Ladle the soup into bowls and scatter the croutons, Serrano chips and basil leaves over before serving.

PEA, BACON & SCAMORZA FRITTATAS

The natural sweetness of peas and zucchini works well with the salty smokiness of bacon and scamorza in these individual frittatas. Scamorza is a type of mozzarella (see page 74) and the smoked version (affumicata) is used here. It can be recognized by its golden-brown rind and unique pear shape, which is due to the way the cheese is hung.

MAKES 4 TO 6   PREPARATION TIME: 15 MINUTES   COOKING TIME: 30 MINUTES

melted butter, for greasing
3 cups Idaho or other baking potatoes
　peeled and cut into ¾ inch chunks
2 teaspoons olive oil
3 slices Canadian bacon, rind removed
　and roughly chopped
2 scallions, green part only,
　finely chopped
1 small zucchini, coarsely grated

⅔ cup frozen petit pois or peas
1 cup diced smoked scamorza
　affumicata cheese
4 tablespoons finely grated Parmesan
　cheese
8 eggs, lightly beaten
sea salt and freshly ground black pepper
crusty bread and tomato salad, to serve

Heat the oven to 375°F. Line four holes of a muffin pan with 6-inch squares of parchment paper, folding the paper to fit the hole; the paper squares should rise above the top of the pan, but might need trimming slightly. Brush the paper cases with a little melted butter. (Alternatively, if not using the paper squares, lightly butter six holes of a muffin pan.)

Cook the potatoes in a pan of boiling salted water for 8 to 10 minutes until tender. Drain them well, then leave to cool in a large bowl.

Meanwhile, heat the olive oil in a large, nonstick skillet over medium heat. Add the bacon and fry for 5 minutes, or until lightly browned and starting to crisp. Using a slotted spoon, remove the bacon and drain on paper towels. Add the scallions and zucchini to the pan and fry, stirring, for 1 minute, or until soft.

Cook the peas in a pan of boiling water until tender, then drain and refresh them under cold running water. Add the peas to the bowl containing the potatoes, along with the bacon, scallions, zucchini, scamorza and Parmesan. Spoon the potato mixture into the prepared paper cases in the muffin pan.

Season the eggs with salt and pepper to taste, then pour into the paper cases, dividing equally. Stir each frittata gently with a fork until all the ingredients are evenly combined. Bake for 20 minutes, or until risen and set. Leave the frittatas in the muffin pan for 5 minutes, then unmold and serve warm or at room temperature, with crusty bread and tomato salad.

Piccalilli

This is one of our bestselling condiments at Bay Tree and it's our take on the classic British version, using some of the core ingredients, but adding an extra twist. This is a must with cold cuts and cheese and it goes particularly well with a really good "raised" pork pie.

**MAKES 3 X 9-OUNCE JARS   PREPARATION TIME: 15 MINUTES, PLUS COOLING
COOKING TIME: 15 MINUTES**

6 tablespoons apple cider vinegar
½ cup sugar
7 tablespoons yellow mustard
½ teaspoon ginger puree
½ teaspoon turmeric
⅔ cup diced carrot
⅔ cup green beans cut into ¾-inch pieces
1 small green bell pepper, seeded and diced
1 small red bell pepper, seeded and diced
1½ tablespoons cornstarch
¾ cup small cauliflower florets

Mix together the vinegar, sugar, mustard, ginger and turmeric in a large, nonreactive pan and bring to a boil. Add the carrot and beans and return to a boil, then stir in the green and red peppers.

Mix the cornstarch into 3 tablespoons water, then stir this into the pan with the cauliflower. Return to a boil, then turn down the heat and simmer for 5 minutes, or until the mixture thickens, but the vegetables remain crunchy.

Remove the pan from the heat and spoon the mixture into sterilized jars while still hot. Cover with lids and leave to cool.

The piccalilli can be eaten once cold but is best left for a few weeks to let the flavors mature and the vegetables soften. Keep in a cool, dark place for up to 4 months, then store in the refrigerator for up to 1 month once opened.

SOUSED MACKEREL WITH
PICCALILLI RÉMOULADE

Reminiscent of days gone by, sousing is simply a form of pickling fish to preserve it. Herring and sardines will work here, too, but whichever type of fish you choose, it must be really fresh.

**SERVES 4   PREPARATION TIME: 20 MINUTES, PLUS OVERNIGHT SOUSING
COOKING TIME: 5 MINUTES**

4 juniper berries, bruised with a knife
½ teaspoon black peppercorns
2 bay leaves
1 teaspoon sea salt
1 teaspoon caraway seeds, toasted
4 shallots, sliced
finely grated zest and juice of 1 lemon
¾ cup plus 2 tablespoons apple cider
   vinegar
½ cup packed light brown sugar
4 mackerel fillets
watercress and rye bread, to serve

PICCALILLI RÉMOULADE:
1⅓ cups peeled celery root, cut into
   thin matchsticks with a mandolin
   or coarsely grated
juice of 1 lemon
1 beet, peeled and grated
5 tablespoons mayonnaise
3 tablespoons Piccalilli (see facing page)
2 tablespoons crème fraîche
   or sour cream
2 tablespoons chopped parsley leaves
sea salt and freshly ground black pepper

Put all the listed ingredients from the juniper berries through the sugar in a saucepan and bring to a boil.

Place the mackerel in a single layer in a nonmetallic shallow dish; they should fit snugly. Pour the hot vinegar mixture over the fish, cover with plastic wrap and leave to cool. The fish will cook slightly in the heat of the vinegar. Once cool, place in the refrigerator and leave the fish overnight to souse (marinate).

Just before serving, make the rémoulade. Toss the prepared celery root in lemon juice to prevent it from discoloring. Combine the celery root with the beet in a serving bowl. Mix together the mayonnaise, piccalilli and crème fraîche with 1 tablespoon warm water. Season to taste with salt and pepper and spoon this dressing over the celery root and beet. Stir until combined, then scatter the parsley over the top.

Remove the mackerel from the sousing liquid and serve with the rémoulade, and with watercress and slices of rye bread on the side.

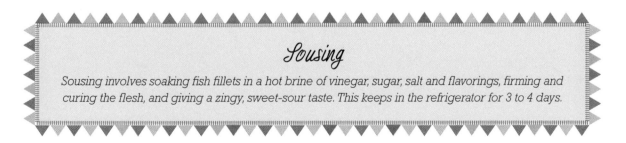

Sousing

Sousing involves soaking fish fillets in a hot brine of vinegar, sugar, salt and flavorings, firming and curing the flesh, and giving a zingy, sweet-sour taste. This keeps in the refrigerator for 3 to 4 days.

FENNEL CARPACCIO & SHRIMP WITH MARINATED OLIVES

This light salad reminds me of summer with its beautiful fresh, invigorating flavors. The quantity of marinated olives is greater than you need for the recipe but they can be kept or up to 1 week in a covered container in the refrigerator.

SERVES 4   PREPARATION TIME: 20 MINUTES, PLUS MARINATING
COOKING TIME: 3 MINUTES

2 teaspoons paprika
18 ounces shelled raw large shrimp,
   thawed if frozen
1 tablespoon olive oil
2 large fennel bulbs, trimmed
2 tablespoons chopped cilantro leaves
sea salt and freshly ground black pepper

MARINATED OLIVES:
finely grated zest and juice of 1 orange
4 tablespoons extra virgin olive oil
1 tablespoon white wine vinegar
1 red chili, seeded and diced
1 large garlic clove, thinly sliced
2 teaspoons fennel seeds, toasted
1½ cups Niçoise olives

To make the olives, strain the orange juice to remove any pulp, then mix with the zest, extra virgin olive oil, vinegar, chili, garlic and fennel seeds. Reserve 3 tablespoons of the marinade to use as a dressing and pour the remaining mixture over the olives. Stir until combined, then leave to marinate for at least 1 hour.

Sprinkle the paprika over the shrimp and season to taste with salt and pepper. Heat the olive oil in a large skillet over medium heat. Add the shrimp and cook for about 3 minutes, or until pink and cooked through. Remove from the pan and leave to cool slightly.

Prepare the salad just before serving. Using a mandolin or a sharp knife, cut the fennel bulbs into thin slices, then put on a serving plate. Top with the shrimp and spoon the reserved dressing over.

Using a slotted spoon, scoop out as many olives as you like. Scatter the olives and cilantro over the top of the salad and serve.

Olives

Olives are too bitter to eat straight from the tree and must be cured to make them edible. Many olives start off green and become black when ripe, although this isn't strictly true of all varieties, of which there are hundreds in various sizes and shades of color, ranging from the Greek purple Kalamata to the French black Niçoise and Spanish green Manzanilla.

WHITE ONION & SAGE FARINATA WITH SPINACH TZATZIKI

Farinata is a thin, savory chickpea-flour cake with the consistency of a crepe. With its origins in Liguria, northwestern Italy, it's so popular bakeries often have a sign in the window to tell customers when the farinata is ready. Usually sold plain, this version is flavored with slices of sweet white onion, olives, chili and sage.

SERVES 4   PREPARATION TIME: 15 MINUTES, PLUS STANDING   COOKING TIME: 25 MINUTES

1⅓ cups chickpea flour
½ teaspoon salt
1 extra-large egg, lightly beaten
5 tablespoons olive oil
1 white onion, thinly sliced
1 red chili, seeded and sliced
½ cup pitted black olives, halved
heaped 1 tablespoon chopped sage

SPINACH TZATZIKI:
7 cups spinach leaves, tough stems
   removed
¾ cup plain yogurt
1 small clove garlic, crushed
1 tablespoon lemon juice
sea salt and freshly ground black pepper

Mix together the chickpea flour and salt in a mixing bowl. Make a well in the middle and stir in the egg, 2 tablespoons of the olive oil and 1¾ cups lukewarm water. Using a wooden spoon, gradually draw the flour into the wet ingredients and stir to make a thick, smooth batter. Cover and leave to stand for 1 hour.

Meanwhile, make the spinach tzatziki. Steam the spinach for 2 minutes, or until it wilts. Drain in a colander, then press the spinach with the back of a wooden spoon to squeeze out any excess water.

Mix together the yogurt, garlic, lemon juice and 4 tablespoons water and season to taste with salt and pepper. Unravel the spinach and stir it into the yogurt mixture. Cover and chill until needed.

Heat the oven to 425°F. Pour the remaining olive oil into a 13- x 9-inch nonstick baking sheet and heat in the oven for 4 minutes, or until very hot. Carefully remove the pan from the oven.

Stir the batter and pour it into the baking pan, then scatter the onion, chili, olives and sage over the top. Bake for 15 to 20 minutes until set and golden. Cut into squares and serve warm with the spinach tzatziki.

Sweet Cherry Tomato & Thyme Pickles

Pickling in sweetened vinegar concentrates the flavor of cherry tomatoes, making them intensely "tomatoey" and succulent. Great with cheeses, pâtés, cold cuts and sandwiches, the pickles also make a stunning gift.

MAKES 2 X 9-OUNCE JARS   PREPARATION TIME: 10 MINUTES, PLUS MARINATING
COOKING TIME: 10 MINUTES

3 tablespoons coriander seeds, slightly crushed
1¾ cups white wine vinegar
2 cups sugar
1 pound 5 ounces mixed vine-ripened yellow and red cherry tomatoes
6 long thyme sprigs

Put the coriander seeds in a small cheesecloth bag in a nonreactive pan with the vinegar and sugar. Bring to a boil, then turn down the heat and simmer, stirring, until the sugar dissolves. Remove the pan from the heat and leave for 30 minutes to infuse.

Meanwhile, prick the tomatoes all over using a wooden toothpick and pack into sterilized jars with the thyme. Remove the cheesecloth bag from the vinegar and pour the vinegar over the tomatoes. Seal the jars.

You can eat the pickles right away, but they are better if left for at least 1 week. Store in a cool, dry, dark place for up to month; once opened, keep in the refrigerator and eat within 2 weeks.

GOAT CHEESE & CHIVE GALETTES WITH
CHERRY TOMATO & THYME PICKLES

The milky acidity of the goat cheese works brilliantly with the sweet-sour flavor of the pickled tomatoes. Served with a crisp green salad, these puff pastry galettes make a delicious summer lunch or a delightful addition to a picnic.

SERVES 4   PREPARATION TIME: 15 MINUTES   COOKING TIME: 20 MINUTES

extra virgin olive oil, for greasing
   and drizzling
11 ounces puff pastry dough sheets,
   thawed if frozen
all-purpose flour, for dusting
10 ounces chèvre blanc or other crumbly
   goat cheese, rind removed
2 garlic cloves, crushed

2 tablespoons snipped chives
1 medium egg, beaten
4 vine-ripened tomatoes, sliced
¼ recipe quantity Sweet Cherry Tomato &
   Thyme Pickles (see facing page), drained
a handful pea shoots
sea salt and freshly ground black pepper
crisp green salad, to serve

Heat the oven to 400°F and grease a large baking sheet. Lay the pastry dough on a lightly floured countertop and cut into four 6½- x 4½-inch rectangles. Score a line about ½ inch in from all the edges.

Crumble the goat cheese into a bowl and stir in the garlic and chives. Season to taste with salt and pepper. Sprinkle the cheese mixture over each piece of dough, leaving the scored border around the edges clear. Brush the edges with a little beaten egg. Place on the baking sheet, top with the sliced tomatoes and drizzle with a little olive oil. Bake for 15 to 20 minutes, or until the pastry is golden. Meanwhile, cut the pickled cherry tomatoes in half. Remove the galettes from the oven and leave to cool slightly. Top each galette with a pile of pea shoots and the pickled tomatoes just before serving hot or cold with a green salad.

Oven-Roasted Tomatoes

These are just so good, and the perfect way to use up a glut of tomatoes.
Slow-roasting concentrates the flavor of the tomatoes and gives them a slightly chewy texture.
You can store them in an airtight container or pack them in a sterilized jar and cover
with olive oil. Use the tomatoes within one month—if they last that long!

**MAKES ABOUT 18 OUNCES   PREPARATION TIME: 15 MINUTES, PLUS DRAINING
COOKING TIME: 2½ HOURS**

2¼ pounds vine-ripened tomatoes, cut in half lengthwise
3 garlic cloves, thinly sliced
4 tablespoons olive oil
6 long oregano sprigs, leaves removed
sea salt and freshly ground black pepper
extra virgin olive oil, to cover (optional)

Using a teaspoon, scoop out the seeds from the tomatoes, leaving a hollow tomato shell. Sprinkle the
inside of each tomato lightly with salt and put, cut-side down, on a wire rack over a baking sheet.
Leave for 1 hour to drain, then rinse and pat dry with paper towels.

Heat the oven to 225°F. Put the tomatoes, cut-side up, on two baking sheets. Sprinkle the tomatoes with
the garlic, olive oil and oregano. Season with a little salt and pepper, then roast the tomatoes for
2 to 2½ hours until they look wrinkly and almost dry. Use right away or leave to cool, then transfer
to an airtight container or pack in a sterilized jar and cover with extra virgin olive oil.
Store in the refrigerator.

CHICKEN BROCHETTES WITH ARTICHOKE & **OVEN-ROASTED TOMATO** CONFIT

Here, skewers of spicy yogurt-coated chicken are served with a piquant vegetable confit. You can use fresh baby artichoke hearts instead of the preserved variety, if you prefer. Discard the leaves and hairy choke, then cook the hearts in boiling salted water until tender.

SERVES 4   PREPARATION TIME: 20 MINUTES, PLUS MARINATING
   COOKING TIME: 30 MINUTES

⅔ cup plain yogurt
1 teaspoon turmeric
2 garlic cloves, crushed
½ red chili, finely chopped
juice of ½ lemon
1¼ pounds boneless, skinless chicken
   breast halves, cut into 16 equal pieces
1 large red onion, cut into wedges
6 large bay leaves, halved lengthwise
olive oil, for brushing
sea salt and freshly ground black pepper
1 tablespoon chopped parsley leaves
ciabatta bread, to serve

ARTICHOKE AND OVEN-ROASTED
   TOMATO CONFIT:
a large pinch saffron threads
4 tablespoons extra virgin olive oil
4 large garlic cloves, sliced
9 ounces roasted artichoke hearts
   in oil (from a jar), drained and
   halved if large
½ recipe quantity Oven-Roasted Tomatoes
   (see page 144)
1 cup pitted Kalamata olives
½ Preserved Lemon (see page 166),
   drained and finely chopped

Mix together the yogurt, turmeric, garlic, chili and lemon juice in a nonmetallic dish. Season to taste with salt and pepper, then add the chicken. Turn the chicken in the yogurt marinade, then leave to marinate, covered, for 1 hour in the refrigerator.

Thread 4 pieces of chicken onto a long, metal skewer, alternating the pieces with a few slices of onion and 3 pieces of bay leaf, starting and ending with onion. Repeat to make 4 skewers in total. Cover and keep in the refrigerator until ready to cook.

To make the confit, soak the saffron threads in 1¼ cups hot water. Heat the extra virgin olive oil in a large skillet and fry the garlic for 1 minute, then add the saffron water and artichokes. Bring to a boil, then turn down the heat to low and simmer for 15 to 20 minutes until the liquid reduces by two-thirds.

Stir in the oven-roasted tomatoes, olives and preserved lemon and simmer for 5 minutes longer, or until the liquid thickens to a saucelike consistency. Add an extra splash of oil and/or water if the confit appears dry. Season to taste with salt and pepper.

Meanwhile, heat the broiler and line the broiler pan with foil. Brush the chicken brochettes with olive oil and broil for 8–10 minutes, turning occasionally, until golden in places and cooked through. Sprinkle the brochettes with parsley and serve with the confit and slices of ciabatta bread.

TAPENADE-STUFFED CHICKEN

We started making olive paste, or tapenade, after a customer asked for it. Our first recipe was so well liked, we started to make additional flavors. This one is delicious as part of an antipasti, mixed into pasta, spooned onto bruschetta or used as a stuffing, as in this recipe.

SERVES 4 (TAPENADE MAKES 3 X 7-OUNCE JARS)   PREPARATION TIME: 20 MINUTES   COOKING TIME: 35 MINUTES

olive oil, for greasing and brushing
4 boneless, skinless chicken breast
  halves, about 6 ounces each
1 cup sliced mozzarella cheese
4 slices San Danielle ham
sea salt and freshly ground black pepper
roasted new potatoes or baked potato
  wedges and green vegetables, such
  as tenderstem broccoli, to serve

MUSHROOM AND OLIVE TAPENADE:
2 cups black olives, pitted and cut into
  wedges
¾ cup green olives, pitted and chopped
2 tablespoons olive oil
1 small onion, diced
2½ cups finely chopped mushrooms
5 tablespoons sun-dried tomato paste
3 large garlic cloves, crushed

To make the tapenade, reserve 1 tablespoon of the black olives, then puree the remainder with the green olives using an immersion blender. Leave to one side.

Heat the olive oil in a skillet and cook the onion over low heat for 10 minutes, or until very soft. Add the mushrooms, tomato paste, garlic and a pinch of black pepper and simmer until any liquid evaporates and the mixture thickens to a paste consistency.

Stir in the olive puree and the reserved whole black olives and simmer for 1 minute longer until heated through. Pack into sterilized jars, cover with lids and leave to cool. Store in the refrigerator and use within 1 month.

Heat the oven to 375°F and lightly grease a baking dish. Make a cut along one side of each chicken breast half to make a long, deep pocket. Spread 1 tablespoon of the tapenade in each pocket and top it with mozzarella. Wrap a slice of ham around each chicken breast to seal in the filling, brush with olive oil and season to taste with salt and pepper.

Put the stuffed chicken breasts in the prepared baking dish and roast for 18 to 20 minutes until cooked through and there is no trace of pink in the middle. Serve with roasted new potatoes and green vegetables.

PERSIAN LAMB CHOPS WITH EGGPLANT CAVIAR & BEET CHIPS

Here, eggplants are roasted until meltingly tender and then mashed with garlic and herbs until smooth and creamy. This "caviar" is delicious with the lamb, coated in a Persian spice mix known as advieh. You might be lucky enough to find heritage beets with their vibrant candy colors of yellow, ruby red and orange to make the chips, in which case all the better.

SERVES 4   PREPARATION TIME: 25 MINUTES   COOKING TIME: 1 HOUR 20 MINUTES

3 uncooked beets, peeled and cut into
⅛-inch-thick slices
2 tablespoons olive oil, plus extra
for brushing
8 to 12 lamb chops, depending on size
sea salt and freshly ground black pepper

EGGPLANT CAVIAR:
2 large eggplants
olive oil, for brushing
6 large garlic cloves
juice of 1 lemon

2 tablespoons extra virgin olive oil
1 handful mint, leaves chopped
1 handful parsley, leaves chopped

PERSIAN SPICE MIX:
2 teaspoons cardamom seeds, about
14 pods
2 teaspoons each coriander seeds, cumin
seeds, turmeric, ground ginger and
dried mint
1 teaspoon grated nutmeg
1 teaspoon salt

Heat the oven to 375°F. Pierce the eggplants all over, then put them in a roasting pan. Brush with olive oil and scatter the garlic around. Roast for 30 minutes, or until the garlic is soft. Remove the garlic from the pan. Turn the eggplants over and return them to the oven to roast for 30 minutes longer. Peel the garlic and mash it into a puree, using the back of a fork. Set aside.

Meanwhile, lightly brush both sides of the beet slices with a little olive oil and season to taste with salt and pepper. Spread out on a baking sheet and roast with the eggplant for 20 to 25 minutes, turning once, until just crisp—they can easily burn and will continue to crisp as they cool. Drain on paper towels and set aside.

Mix together all the ingredients for the spice mix, then rub over both sides of the lamb chops. Save any leftover spice mix in an airtight container for future use. Remove the eggplants from the oven and leave until cool enough to handle.

Heat the olive oil in a large skillet over high heat and sear the lamb chops in two or three batches, depending on the size of your pan, for 2 minutes on each side until golden brown. As they are seared, transfer the chops to a large roasting pan. Place in the oven and roast for about 5 minutes; the lamb will still be pink in the middle.

Meanwhile, peel the eggplants, then chop the flesh. Add to the bowl with the roasted garlic and mash to a puree. Stir in the lemon juice and extra virgin olive oil and season to taste with salt and pepper. Fold in the herbs. Serve the "caviar" topped with the lamb chops and scatter the beet chips around.

BEEF, PORCINI & CHESTNUT BOURGUIGNON

This is a rich, comforting stew, packed with flavor from the dried porcini mushrooms, red wine, garlic, stock and beef. Creamy mashed potatoes are a must for soaking up the meaty gravy.

SERVES 4   PREPARATION TIME: 20 MINUTES, PLUS SOAKING   COOKING TIME: 2½ HOURS

½ ounce dried porcini mushrooms
2 tablespoons olive oil
1 pound 10 ounces braising beef, trimmed of fat and cut into large pieces
1¼ cups peeled shallots, halved if large
3 garlic cloves, chopped
2 tablespoons all-purpose flour
1½ cups red wine
½ cup good-quality beef stock

9 ounces cremini mushrooms, halved if large
6 thyme sprigs
1 bay leaf
½-inch strip pared unwaxed orange zest
1¼ cups canned cooked chestnuts, halved
1 tablespoon Worcestershire sauce
sea salt and freshly ground black pepper

Soak the porcini mushrooms in 6 tablespoons hot water for 20 minutes, or until soft. Drain the porcini, reserving the soaking liquid.

Heat half the olive oil in a large Dutch oven over medium heat. Season the beef to taste with salt and pepper, then sear it in two or three batches until brown all over, adding more oil when necessary. Using a slotted spoon, remove the beef from the pan and leave to one side. Add the shallots, cover and fry, stirring occasionally, for 10 minutes, or until soft. Add the garlic and cook for 1 minute longer.

Return the seared beef to the pot. Stir in the flour and cook for a couple of minutes, stirring. Pour in the wine and deglaze by scraping up any bits stuck to the bottom of the pot. Let the wine bubble gently for 5 minutes, or until reduced. Add the porcini and their soaking liquid, the stock, cremini mushrooms, thyme, bay leaf and orange zest and bring to a boil. Turn down the heat and simmer, partially covered and stirring occasionally, for 1¼ hours.

Add the chestnuts and Worcestershire sauce. Cover and simmer for 30 to 40 minutes longer until the beef is extremely tender and the sauce has thickened. Add more stock during this time if the stew appears dry, or cook uncovered if there is too much sauce. Season to taste with salt and pepper and serve.

Dried Mushrooms

Dried mushrooms, such as porcini, shiitake and morels, keep for ages and, after briefly rehydrating in hot water, they add an intense flavor to all sorts of dishes.

SEAFOOD & RED PEPPER TAGINE

Roasting caramelizes the natural sugars in red peppers, as well as concentrating their flavor and lending a slight smokiness. Long, pointed romano red peppers work well here, but you can use regular large bell peppers instead, if preferred.

SERVES 4   PREPARATION TIME: 20 MINUTES, PLUS MARINATING
COOKING TIME: 55 MINUTES

2 romano or other large red bell peppers
2 teaspoons ground cumin
1 tablespoon ground coriander
3 garlic cloves, crushed
juice of 1 lime
1¼ pounds thick, skinless fillets of white
    fish, such as pollock, cod, haddock
    or monkfish, cut into large bite-size
    pieces
9 ounces raw shelled large shrimp
14 ounces new potatoes, halved
    or quartered if large
2 tablespoons olive oil

1 onion, sliced
2-inch piece fresh gingerroot, peeled and
    grated
4 long thyme sprigs
1 can (15-oz.) crushed tomatoes
1 cup plus 2 tablespoons good-quality
    fish stock
1 teaspoon harissa paste, or to taste
½ cup Niçoise olives
sea salt and freshly ground black pepper
couscous, cilantro leaves and lime
    wedges, to serve

Heat the oven to 400°F. Put the red peppers on a baking sheet lined with parchment paper and roast for 35 to 40 minutes until soft. Put the peppers in a plastic bag and leave for 5 minutes, which will make the skins easier to remove. Remove the pepper skin and seeds, then slice the flesh and leave to one side.

Meanwhile, mix together the cumin, coriander, garlic and lime juice with salt and pepper to taste in a large, nonmetallic dish. Add the fish and shrimp and turn to coat them in the marinade. Leave to marinate, covered, in the refrigerator for 30 minutes.

Cook the potatoes in a saucepan of boiling salted water for 10 to 15 minutes until tender. Drain the potatoes and leave them to one side.

Heat the olive oil in a large Dutch oven or saucepan over medium heat. Add the onion, cover the pan and cook for 8 minutes, or until soft. Add the ginger and thyme and cook for 1 minute longer. Pour in the tomatoes and stock and bring to a boil. Stir in the harissa, then turn down the heat and simmer, stirring occasionally, for 10 minutes, or until reduced.

Remove the fish and shrimp from the marinade and stir the marinade into the pot with the roasted peppers, potatoes and olives. Gently stir in the fish, cover and simmer for 8 minutes, then put the shrimp on top and simmer for 3 to 4 minutes longer until they are pink and cooked through. Serve with couscous alongside, with cilantro scattered over and wedges of lime for squeezing over.

Butternut & Ginger Curd

It might seem unusual to use butternut squash in a sweet preserve, but this is sublime and has just the right amount of ginger to give a little zing without being overpowering. The squash also gives the curd the most vibrant golden color.

MAKES 3 X 9-OUNCE JARS   PREPARATION TIME: 15 MINUTES   COOKING TIME: 40 MINUTES

4¼ cups peeled, seeded and chopped butternut squash (1 small squash weighing about 1 pound 5 ounces)
finely grated zest and juice of 1 lemon and 1 orange
5 tablespoons unsalted butter, cubed
1 cup sugar
2 extra-large eggs, plus 2 egg yolks, lightly beaten and strained
4 pieces preserved ginger in syrup, diced, plus 3 tablespoons of the syrup

Put the squash in a pan with ½ cup water and bring to a boil, then turn down the heat and simmer for 10 minutes, or until tender. Drain well and leave the squash in the colander to dry. Press the squash through a strainer to make a smooth puree; discard any fibers left in the strainer.

Measure 1½ cups of the squash puree and put it in a heatproof bowl. Add the citrus zests and juices, butter, sugar and eggs and mix together. Set the bowl over a pan of gently simmering water, making sure the bottom doesn't touch the water. Stir as the butter melts and the sugar dissolves, then heat the mixture to 185°F, stirring regularly, until it thickens to a curd consistency. This will take 25 to 30 minutes. Take care you don't overheat the mixture, because you don't want the eggs to scramble.

Stir the preserved ginger and syrup into the curd, then pour into sterilized jars, cover with lids and leave to cool. The curd will keep for up to 2 weeks in the refrigerator.

BUTTERNUT & GINGER CURD RAVIOLI WITH ROMANO

This recipe is a delicious twist on the classic pumpkin-filled pasta. The ravioli are served with a simple butter and sage sauce and finished off with a sprinkling of grated romano. Use "00" flour, which is extra fine and always recommended when making fresh pasta. You can replace the Butternut & Ginger Curd with mashed roasted butternut squash mixed with 1 teaspoon finely chopped rosemary, if preferred. When serving, spoon the pasta onto serving plates and top with the sauce, rather than tipping the pasta into the sauce.

SERVES 4   PREPARATION TIME: 40 MINUTES, PLUS RESTING   COOKING TIME: 15 MINUTES

2¼ cups "00" flour, plus extra for dusting
½ teaspoon salt
2 eggs, plus 2 yolks
fine semolina, for dusting
7 tablespoons butter
2 to 3 tablespoons chopped sage,
   to taste
sea salt and freshly ground black pepper

FILLING:
6 tablespoons Butternut & Ginger Curd
   (see facing page)
5 tablespoons very finely ground
   blached almonds
6 tablespoons fresh white bread crumbs
4 tablespoons finely grated romano
   cheese, plus extra to serve
2 tablespoons ricotta cheese

To make the pasta, sift the flour into a large mixing bowl. Mix in the salt and make a well in the middle. Lightly beat the eggs and egg yolks together in a separate bowl. Add half the beaten eggs to the flour and mix in using your fingers, then gradually add the remaining egg as needed, until the mixture comes together to make a ball of dough.

Lightly dust the countertop with flour and knead the pasta dough for 3 minutes, or until smooth, silky and elastic. Wrap the dough in plastic wrap and leave to rest in the refrigerator for at least 30 minutes. (It can be kept for up to 1 day in the refrigerator.)

Meanwhile, mix together all the ingredients for the filling. Season to taste with salt and pepper. Cover with plastic wrap and leave in the refrigerator until ready to use.

Line two baking sheets with parchment paper and sprinkle with semolina. Dust the countertop with flour again. Cut the ball of dough in half and wrap one half in the plastic wrap to prevent it from drying out.

Take the other piece of dough, flatten it slightly and pass it through the widest setting of a pasta machine. Fold the dough over and pass it through again on the same setting. Repeat this process six times until you have a rectangular piece of dough. This will knead the dough. Repeat with the second piece of dough, then wrap them in plastic wrap again.

To roll out the pasta, start with the pasta machine at its widest setting and pass the dough through the rollers. Repeat this process, passing the dough twice through each setting before turning it down by a grade.

CONTINUED ON PAGE **158**

Lightly dust the dough with flour if it is a little sticky, and cut it in half crosswise if it becomes too long to manage. Keep the rolled-out dough covered with a dry, clean dish towel to prevent it from drying out.

After passing the dough through the final setting, lay the fine sheet of pasta on the floured countertop. Using a 2¼-inch round cutter, mark out circles where the parcels will be; don't cut through the pasta at this point.

Put a teaspoon of filling in the middle of each circle, then lightly brush around the filling with water. Lay a second sheet of pasta on top, pressing around each lump of filling and squeezing out any air bubbles.

Use the round cutter to cut out the ravioli and seal the edges. To avoid them having thick edges, press the edges together with your fingers, pinching the dough all the way around the filling. Put the ravioli on the prepared baking sheets. Repeat until you have used all the dough and filling. The mixture will make about 40 ravioli. Heat the oven to 100°F.

Cook the ravioli in four batches in a large saucepan of boiling salted water for about 3 minutes until the pasta is al dente. Using a flat slotted spoon, remove the ravioli from the water and keep warm in two covered shallow bowls in the low oven.

Meanwhile, melt the butter in a large skillet. Add the chopped sage and heat through for 1 minute. Stir in 6 tablespoons of the pasta cooking water and season to taste with salt and pepper. Serve the pasta in large shallow bowls, coated in the butter sauce and sprinkled with extra romano cheese.

Fresh Pasta

Making fresh egg pasta is immensely satisfying. All you need is a pasta machine (and even that isn't always necessary), the right type of flour and fresh eggs. Tipo "00" is an extra-fine flour traditionally used for egg pasta. It's sometimes combined with semolina, which gives the pasta extra "bite." The amount of added semolina varies, depending on personal preference, as does the quantity of egg, which is what gives the pasta a silky richness.

When cooking pasta, the Italians often say "pasta likes friends," which means you have to keep an eye on it. Cooking the pasta in plenty of water at a rolling boil is a must, and the water is meant to be as "salty as the sea." Don't overcrowd the pan, because the pasta can stick together—there should be enough water to allow the pasta to bobble about. Egg pasta is traditionally served in the north of Italy with buttery, creamy sauces.

MUSHROOM PÂTÉ EN CROÛTE WITH RED ONION RELISH

This relish is particularly good with pâté, cheeses and meats, hot and cold, and is a real favorite on my homemade pizzas. The mushroom pâté, wrapped in puff pastry, can be served as a vegetarian lunch or as part of a picnic—either way don't forget a spoonful of the relish.

SERVES 6   PREPARATION TIME: 30 MINUTES, PLUS SOAKING   COOKING TIME: 1 HOUR

1 ounce dried porcini mushrooms
4 tablespoons cashew nuts
1 tablespoon olive oil
1 onion, finely chopped
3 garlic cloves, chopped
3½ cups chopped cremini mushrooms
2 teaspoons dried thyme
5 tablespoons fresh bread crumbs
2 tablespoons dark soy sauce
1 carrot, finely grated
11 ounces puff pastry dough sheets, thawed if frozen

all-purpose flour, for dusting
1 medium egg, lightly beaten
sea salt and freshly ground black pepper

RED ONION RELISH:
2¼ pounds red onions, thinly sliced
¾ cup plus 2 tablespoons red wine vinegar
2 cloves
½ teaspoon ground cinnamon
1⅓ cups packed light brown sugar
2 tablespoons lemon juice

Pour just enough hot water over the porcini to cover and leave for 20 minutes, or until soft. Toast the cashews in a large dry skillet for 3 to 5 minutes, turning once, until pale golden. Leave to cool.

Heat the olive oil in the skillet and cook the onion, covered, for 5 minutes, or until soft. Add the garlic, cremini mushrooms and thyme and cook, stirring regularly, for 5 minutes longer, or until tender. Drain the porcini, reserving 4 tablespoons of the soaking liquid; squeeze out any excess water and roughly chop. Add the porcini to the pan, stir and cook for 5 minutes longer. Transfer the filling mixture to a bowl.

Heat the oven to 400°F. Finely chop the toasted cashews in a food processor, then tip them into the bowl containing the mushroom mixture. Stir in the bread crumbs, reserved soaking liquid, soy sauce and carrot. The mixture should be like a coarse pâté. Season to taste with salt and pepper.

Lay the pastry dough on a lightly floured countertop and spoon the mushroom mixture down the middle. Draw up the long sides of the dough over the filling, trim off any excess and wet the edges. Press together and crimp to seal. Use the trimmings to decorate the seam. Brush with beaten egg and prick the top a few times with a fork. Transfer to a baking sheet and bake for 40 to 45 minutes until the pastry is golden.

For the relish, put the onions, vinegar and spices in a nonreactive saucepan. Bring to a boil, then turn down the heat and simmer, covered, for 20 to 30 minutes, stirring occasionally, until the onions are soft. Stir in the sugar and lemon juice and return to a boil, then simmer until thick. Pack into sterilized jars, cover with lids and cool. Store in a cool, dry, dark place for up to 6 months; once opened, keep in the refrigerator. Serve the mushroom pâté in slices with the relish.

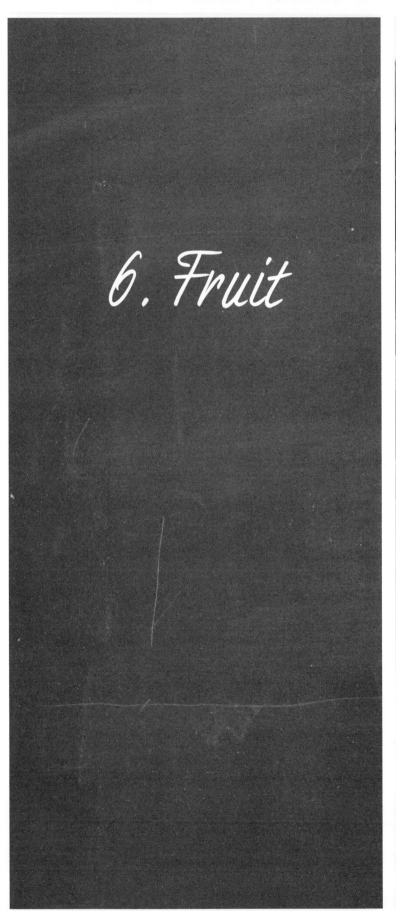

6. Fruit

MOROCCAN CHICKEN PATTIES WITH DATE CONFIT

Each of these diminutive spiced chicken patties is served on a lettuce leaf with red onion and cilantro, topped with a spoonful of sweet chili-hot confit. Serve as a light meal with couscous and salad, or as canapés.

SERVES 4   PREPARATION TIME: 25 MINUTES, PLUS SOAKING   COOKING TIME: 50 MINUTES

1 pound 5 ounces boneless, skinless chicken breast halves

4 garlic cloves, finely chopped

1-inch piece fresh gingerroot, peeled and grated

2 teaspoons ras el hanout

3 tablespoons olive oil

½ teaspoon light brown sugar

TO SERVE:

16 small hearts of lettuce leaves

4-inch piece English cucumber, quartered lengthwise, seeded and diced

1 small red onion, finely chopped

1 handful cilantro leaves

DATE CONFIT:

20 ready-to-eat pitted dates, halved

1 tablespoon olive oil

2 shallots, chopped

½ teaspoon ground cinnamon

1 Thai chili, finely chopped

1 teaspoon light brown sugar

2 tablespoons pomegranate molasses

sea salt and freshly ground black pepper

First make the date confit. Put the dates in a bowl, cover with just-boiled water and leave for 1 hour. Meanwhile, heat the olive oil in a skillet and fry the shallots, covered, for 20 to 25 minutes until very soft.

Drain the dates and add them to the pan, squashing them with the back of a fork to break them down. Stir in 4 tablespoons water, the cinnamon, chili and sugar and cook for 5 minutes longer, or until it forms a thick jam consistency. Add more water if it is too thick. Stir in the pomegranate molasses and season to taste with salt and pepper. You can blend the mixture if you prefer a smoother consistency. Spoon the confit into a serving bowl and leave to cool.

Meanwhile, heat the oven to 100°F. Grind the chicken in a food processor, then stir in the garlic, ginger and ras el hanout. Season to taste with salt and pepper. Form the chicken mixture into 16 equal balls, the size of golf balls. Flatten each one to make a little patty.

Heat two-thirds of the oil in a large, nonstick skillet over medium heat. Fry the patties, in two or three batches, if necessary, for 3 minutes on each side. Just before they finish cooking on each side, sprinkle with a little sugar and cook until slightly caramelized. Drain on paper towels and keep warm in the low oven while you cook the remaining patties, adding more oil when necessary.

To serve, put a chicken patty on top of each lettuce leaf, scatter a little cucumber, red onion and cilantro over and top with a spoonful of the date confit. Serve warm or at room temperature.

Raspberry Vinegar

This fruit-infused, ruby-red vinegar is so versatile: add it to dressings; use it to deglaze a pan after browning meat; or mix it into sparkling water to make a refreshing drink. Soups and stews also benefit from a splash of this sweet-sour condiment. Flavored vinegars require a minimum of effort to prepare, yet a bottle makes an indispensable addition to every cook's supply of ingredients.

MAKES 2 X 9-OUNCE BOTTLES   PREPARATION TIME: 10 MINUTES, PLUS 3 DAYS MACERATING AND AT LEAST 1 WEEK MATURING   COOKING TIME: 5 MINUTES

2 cups white wine vinegar
½ cup plus 1 tablespoon sugar
9 ounces raspberries

Bring the vinegar to a boil in a nonreactive pan and leave to bubble away for 2 minutes. Remove from the heat and stir in the sugar until dissolved. Transfer to a heatproof bowl and leave to cool to 105°F.

Add the raspberries to the bowl and stir well, crushing the fruit slightly with the back of a fork. Cover and leave in a cool place to macerate for 3 days, stirring occasionally.

After 3 days, strain the vinegar through a jelly bag, or a piece of cheesecloth, into a measuring jug, then pour into sterilized bottles. Seal and leave for at least a week before use. The vinegar will keep for up to 6 months stored in a cool, dry, dark place.

LAMB, BEET & PUY LENTIL SALAD WITH
RASPBERRY VINEGAR DRESSING

The combined qualities of a slightly syrupy texture and a fruity flavor mean raspberry vinegar is not only excellent in the dressing for this salad, but also works as a glaze for the lamb. If you aren't making your own raspberry vinegar, be sure to buy a good-quality one.

SERVES 4   PREPARATION TIME: 20 MINUTES, PLUS RESTING   COOKING TIME: 35 MINUTES

heaped ¾ cup Puy lentils
1 tablespoon good-quality concentrated
   chicken stock
4 thick boneless lamb loin chops, about
   6 ounces each
1 tablespoon olive oil
1 tablespoon Raspberry Vinegar
   (see facing page)
4 handfuls baby spinach leaves
2 cups diced drained cooked beets
   in natural juice

2 scallions, thinly sliced
1 long celery rib, thinly sliced
3 tablespoons chopped parsley leaves

RASPBERRY VINEGAR DRESSING:
3 tablespoons extra virgin olive oil
2 tablespoons Raspberry Vinegar
   (see facing page)
heaped 1 teaspoon honey
1 teaspoon Dijon mustard
sea salt and freshly ground black pepper

Cover the lentils with ¾ inch water and bring to a boil. Add the chicken stock and stir well, then turn down the heat and simmer, partially covered, for 30 minutes, or until tender. Drain well and leave to one side.

Meanwhile, make the raspberry vinegar dressing. Put all the ingredients in a screw-top jar and shake until combined. Season to taste with salt and pepper.

Brush both sides of the lamb with the olive oil and season to taste with salt and pepper. Heat a large skillet over high heat and sear the lamb for 2 minutes on each side, or until golden brown. Turn down the heat to medium, add the vinegar and turn the lamb briefly until it is coated in the vinegar, oil and pan juices, but remains pink in the middle. Remove the lamb from the pan and put it on a warm plate. Cover with foil and leave to rest for 10 minutes.

Put a handful of spinach on each serving plate and top with the lentils, beets, scallions and celery. Cut the lamb into slices and arrange on the salad. Spoon the dressing over and toss lightly to combine, then sprinkle the parsley over before serving.

Preserved Lemons

If you haven't cooked with preserved lemons before, they are fantastic for sprucing up casseroles with a Middle Eastern or North African slant, mixing into a rub, or adding to a stuffing for meat and fish or a dressing. They have an intense salty, citrus flavor, so use in moderate amounts.

**MAKES A 2-CUP JAR   PREPARATION TIME: 20 MINUTES, PLUS 2 WEEKS INFUSING
COOKING TIME: 5 MINUTES**

⅔ cup white wine vinegar
¼ cup salt
¼ cup sugar
6 unwaxed lemons
½ teaspoon yellow mustard seeds
½ teaspoon coriander seeds
2 long red chilies

Put the vinegar, salt, sugar and 3 tablespoons water in a nonreactive pan. Bring to a boil, stirring until the salt and sugar dissolve. Boil for a minute longer, then remove the pan from the heat and leave to cool.

Squeeze 2 the lemons and add the juice to the cooling mixture. Cut the remaining lemons into ¼-inch-thick slices, discarding the ends.

Line the side of a sterilized jar with 4 of the best lemon slices, making sure they fit tightly together. Cut the remaining lemon slices into quarters. Put them in a bowl and stir in the mustard and coriander seeds. Pack the quartered lemon slices and spices into the jar with the chilies.

Add the vinegar mixture to cover the lemons. Cover and leave for 2 weeks before use. Store in a cool, dry, dark place for up to 2 months. Once opened, keep in the refrigerator.

PRESERVED LEMON-STUFFED SARDINES WITH GARLIC–YOGURT SAUCE

Finely chopped preserved lemon is combined with herbs, spices and bread crumbs to make a fragrant stuffing for fresh sardines. Mackerel and herring would both make suitable alternatives to the sardines.

SERVES 4   PREPARATION TIME: 15 MINUTES   COOKING TIME: 18 MINUTES

olive oil, for greasing and drizzling
8 to 12 sardines, depending on their size, dressed and head removed if preferred
watercress salad and crusty bread, to serve

PRESERVED LEMON STUFFING:
¾ cup fresh white bread crumbs
¼ to ⅓ cup finely chopped Preserved Lemons (see facing page). If using bought preserved lemons, scrape away and discard the flesh and finely chop the peel

1 teaspoon paprika
1 teaspoon ground coriander
½ red chili, seeded and finely chopped
2 tablespoons olive oil
1 small handful parsley leaves, chopped
1 small handful of mint leaves, chopped
sea salt and freshly ground black pepper

GARLIC–YOGURT SAUCE:
⅔ cup plain yogurt
1 garlic clove, crushed
juice of ½ lemon
2 tablespoons chopped mint leaves

Heat the oven to 400°F and lightly grease a baking dish large enough to hold the sardines in a single layer. Rinse the sardines inside and out, then pat dry with paper towels. Mix together all the ingredients for the stuffing and season to taste with salt and pepper.

Using a teaspoon, spoon the stuffing into the sardines, pressing it into the cavity of each fish.

Put the sardines in the prepared baking dish, drizzle over a little more olive oil and season to taste with salt and pepper. Bake for 16 to 18 minutes until the sardines are cooked and the stuffing is heated through.

Meanwhile, make the garlic–yogurt sauce. Mix together the yogurt, garlic and lemon juice in a serving bowl, then season to taste with salt and pepper and sprinkle the mint over the top.

Serve the sardines with the yogurt sauce, a watercress salad and crusty bread.

DUCK WITH CHERRY & FIVE-SPICE SAUCE

Frozen cherries are perfect for this Chinese-spiced sauce, because they break down when cooked into a rich, dark sauce, and they conveniently come pitted. Look for the dark, juicy morello cherries and don't bother thawing them before cooking.

SERVES 4   PREPARATION TIME: 15 MINUTES   COOKING TIME: 35 MINUTES

splash of olive oil
4 duck breast halves, skin on
jasmine rice and finely chopped scallions,
   to serve

CHERRY AND FIVE-SPICE SAUCE:
1 tablespoon olive oil
1 shallot, diced
1-inch piece fresh gingerroot,
   peeled and grated

1⅔ cups frozen dark cherries,
   preferably morello
1 teaspoon Chinese five-spice powder
finely grated zest and juice of 1 small
   orange
1 tablespoon lemon juice
1 teaspoon cornstarch
sea salt and freshly ground black pepper

To make the sauce, heat the olive oil in a saucepan over medium heat and fry the shallot for 5 minutes, or until soft. Add the ginger and cook for 1 minute longer, then add the cherries, Chinese five-spice, orange zest and juice and lemon juice. Bring to a boil, then turn down the heat and simmer, stirring occasionally, for 8 minutes, or until the cherries soften and start to break down.

Mix the cornstarch with 1 teaspoon water, stir it into the sauce and cook for 5 minutes longer, or until it reduces and thickens. Season to taste with salt and pepper and leave to cool slightly. Blend the sauce with an immersion blender or mash, depending on whether you prefer a smooth or slightly chunky sauce.

Heat the oven to 375°F. Heat a splash of oil in a large, nonstick skillet over high heat. Put the duck breasts in the pan, skin-side down, and sear for 4 minutes, or until the skins are crisp. Transfer to a roasting pan, skin-side up, and roast for 8 to 10 minutes until cooked through, but still pink in the middle.

Slice the duck and serve with jasmine rice sprinkled with scallions and the cherry sauce. Any remaining sauce will keep in a sterilized jar for up to 2 weeks in the refrigerator.

Fruit Sauces

I'm all for using fruit in savory dishes, especially as the base of a sauce, but it's best to stick to classic combinations. Fruit that has a slight acidity works best in savory dishes, such as cherries, apples, blackberries, blueberries, citrus fruit, rhubarb and even raspberries, helping to cut through the richness of meat, poultry and game.

Orange, Coriander & Thyme Jam

In contrast to the slight bitterness of a marmalade made with Seville oranges (delicious as it is), this orange jam has a fresher, sweeter citrus flavor. It is infused with fresh thyme and the slightly lemony tang of coriander seeds. To make ginger jam, you can replace the thyme with two pieces of drained, finely chopped preserved ginger in syrup.

**MAKES 2 X 1¼-CUP JARS   PREPARATION TIME: 15 MINUTES,
PLUS OVERNIGHT SOAKING   COOKING TIME: 2 HOURS**

3 tablespoons coriander seeds
2¼ pounds unwaxed oranges, such as Valencia or Navel, washed and cut in half
2 lemons, washed and cut in half
4¼ cups plus 2 tablespoons sugar
4 tablespoons thyme leaves

Toast the coriander seeds in a dry skillet over medium heat for about 3 minutes until they start to smell aromatic. Leave to cool, then roughly crush using a mortar and pestle. Leave to one side.

Squeeze the orange and lemon juices and strain into a large bowl, reserving the contents of the strainer. Using a spoon, scrape out the pith and membrane from the skins into a bowl, then add the strainer contents.

Thinly slice the peel from 2 of the oranges and add it to the juice. Roughly chop the remaining orange peel and add to the bowl with the seeds. Tip the seeds, membrane, lemon peel and roughly chopped orange peel into the middle of a large square of cheesecloth. Scatter the toasted coriander seeds over and twist the cheesecloth, tying a knot in the top to make a bag.

Pour the juice into a preserving kettle or stainless-steel saucepan with 7½ cups water. Add the cheesecloth bag, pressing it down to submerge it in the liquid, then leave, covered, overnight.

The next day, bring the liquid in the pan to a boil, then turn down the heat and simmer for 1½ hours until the peel is really soft and the liquid has reduced by half. Squeeze out any liquid from the bag, then remove and discard it.

Add the sugar and stir until it dissolves. Increase the heat and bring the mixture to a rapid, rolling boil. Boil for 15 minutes, or until thick. To test for doneness, use a jelly or candy thermometer (it should register 225°F). Or put a teaspoonful of the orange jelly onto a cold saucer and leave it to cool for a few minutes, then push it with your finger; if the jam wrinkles, it is ready. Stir in the thyme, then pack into sterilized jars and seal. Store in a cool, dry, dark place for up to a year. Once opened, keep in the refrigerator and eat within 1 month.

ROAST GUINEA FOWL GLAZED WITH
ORANGE, CORIANDER & THYME JAM

The fresh, citrusy flavor of the jelly is great with guinea fowl, giving the skin a wonderful golden glaze and imparting a delicious sweetness to the gravy.

SERVES 4   PREPARATION TIME: 25 MINUTES   COOKING TIME: 1 HOUR 35 MINUTES

1 guinea fowl, about 3¾ pounds,
   thawed if frozen
2 tablespoons Orange, Coriander
   & Thyme Jam (see page 170)
1 large parsnip
6 tablespoons sunflower oil
1¼ cups good-quality chicken stock

LEMON AND HERB STUFFING:
3 tablespoons butter
1 onion, finely chopped
1½ cups fresh white bread crumbs
1 tablespoon thyme leaves
1 tablespoon chopped flat-leaf parsley
finely grated zest of 1 lemon
salt and freshly ground black pepper

Heat the oven to 350°F. Rinse the guinea fowl and pat dry with paper towels. Leave to one side while you make the stuffing.

Melt the butter in a skillet over low heat and fry the onion, stirring occasionally, for 8 minutes, or until soft. Remove the pan from the heat and stir in the bread crumbs, herbs and lemon zest, then season to taste with salt and pepper.

Loosely stuff the guinea fowl with the lemon and herb stuffing, then put it on a rack over a roasting pan containing about 1 inch water. Using your hands, smear the jam all over the guinea fowl until it is completely covered, then tie the legs together with a piece of string.

Roast the guinea fowl for 1¼ hours, basting with the juices in the pan halfway through. Test for doneness by inserting a skewer into the thickest part of the leg—the juices should run clear. If not, return the guinea fowl to the oven to roast for 10 minutes longer.

Meanwhile, using a vegetable peeler, slice the parsnip into long, thin strips. Heat the sunflower oil in a skillet over medium-high heat and fry the parsnip in two or three batches for a few minutes until the strips are crisp and golden. Drain on paper towels.

When the guinea fowl is cooked through, transfer it to a warm plate, cover loosely with foil and leave to rest. Reduce the oven temperature to 200°F and put the parsnip strips into the oven to keep warm while you make the gravy.

Spoon off any surplus fat from the roasting pan, then add the stock and bring to a boil on the stovetop, stirring to loosen any bits stuck to the bottom and sides of the pan. Season to taste with salt and pepper, then boil until the gravy reduces and thickens. Carve the guinea fowl and serve with the stuffing, gravy and parsnip strips.

SLOW-COOKED PORK WITH APPLES & CIDER SAUCE

Instead of serving the pork roasted in the conventional way, in this recipe the meat is cooked long and slow in a fruity hard-cider sauce. A spoonful of red-currant jelly adds just the right amount of sweetness and color to the dish.

SERVES 4 TO 6   PREPARATION TIME: 20 MINUTES   COOKING TIME: 3½ HOURS

1 boneless pork leg (fresh ham) or Boston butt roast, about 2 pounds 7 ounces, skin scored
1 tablespoon olive oil
2 onions, thickly sliced
1 carrot, thickly sliced
4 garlic cloves, sliced
2 rosemary sprigs, leaves removed
1 bay leaf

1¼ cups hard cider or apple juice
1 cup good-quality chicken stock
2 apples, each cored and cut into 8 wedges
2 teaspoons red-currant jelly
2 teaspoons soft butter
2 teaspoons all-purpose flour
sea salt and freshly ground black pepper

Heat the oven to 325°F. To make cracklings, cut off the skin and adjoining fat from the pork roast. Put it in a baking dish and pour over just-boiled water; this helps to open the cuts in the skin. Drain well, pat dry and season generously with salt and pepper, then leave to one side until ready to cook.

Heat the olive oil in a large Dutch oven and brown the pork for 2 minutes on each side until colored all over. Remove from the pot and leave to one side.

Add the onions and carrot to the Dutch oven and cook for 3 minutes, stirring occasionally, then stir in the garlic, rosemary and bay leaf. Return the pork to the pot and pour in the cider and chicken stock. Bring to a boil, cover with the lid and transfer the pot to the oven. Cook for 2¼ hours, then remove from the oven and add the apples around the pork. Return the pot to the oven to cook for 45 minutes longer. At the same time put the pork skin in the oven.

Remove the Dutch oven from the oven. Transfer the pork and apples to a warm plate, cover with foil and leave to rest. Increase the oven temperature to 425°F to crisp the cracklings while the pork rests and you make the sauce.

Skim the fat from the surface of the cooking liquid in the pot, then strain into a saucepan, pressing down on the vegetables to remove as much liquid as possible. Stir in the red-currant jelly and bring to a boil, then lightly boil for 10 minutes, or until the sauce reduces by half.

Meanwhile, mix together the butter and flour to make a paste. Reduce the heat to low and stir the paste into the sauce, a little at a time. Season to taste with salt and pepper, then simmer, stirring, until the sauce thickens. Slice the pork and cracklings and serve with the sauce spooned over and the apples on the side.

Lemon Curd

One of my favorite desserts is homemade lemon meringue pie, so when I developed this recipe the aim was to create a curd that could double as a pie or cake filling, as well as make a delicious preserve. The result is a curd with a really gutsy, zingy lemon flavor combined with a rich, creamy texture—it's always a big hit with my family!

MAKES 3 X ¾-CUP JARS   PREPARATION TIME: 10 MINUTES   COOKING TIME: 15 MINUTES

finely grated zest of 1 lemon
juice of 3 lemons
⅔ cup plus 1 tablespoon butter
1¼ cups sugar
4 eggs

Put the lemon zest and juice in a nonreactive saucepan with the butter and sugar. Warm over low heat, stirring until the butter melts and the sugar dissolves, then remove the pan from the heat.

Beat the eggs using an immersion blender until combined, then beat them into the butter mixture. Return the pan to low heat and cook for about 5 minutes, stirring continuously with a wooden spoon, until the mixture thickens to a custard-sauce consistency and any white foam on the top disappears. Make sure the mixture does not boil, because the eggs could curdle.

Remove the pan from the heat. Pour the curd into sterilized jars and seal. Leave the curd to cool, then store in the refrigerator. The curd will keep for up to 2 weeks.

LEMON CURD–MERINGUE SEMIFREDDO

This takes all my favorite bits from a lemon meringue pie and transforms them into a deliciously indulgent, creamy dessert. Semifreddo is not quite an ice cream, because you don't have to churn it, but it's just as good, and, as its name suggests, it's semi-frozen so you can take it out of the freezer just before serving. You won't need all of the meringues—save the rest for another day to serve with softly whipped cream—or use bought meringues.

**SERVES 8 TO 10   PREPARATION TIME: 30 MINUTES, PLUS 5 HOURS FREEZING
COOKING TIME: 1¼ HOURS**

2 extra-large eggs, separated
½ cup plus 2 tablespoons sugar
grated zest of 1 large lemon, plus extra
   to serve
½ cup Lemon Curd (see facing page)
1¼ cups heavy cream

MERINGUES (MAKES 8):
2 extra-large egg whites at room
   temperature
¼ cup superfine sugar
½ cup confectioners' sugar

Heat the oven to 225°F and line two baking sheets with parchment paper. First, make the meringues. Using a hand-held electric mixer on medium speed, beat the egg whites in a large, greasefree bowl until they will form stiff peaks. Turn up the speed and gradually add the superfine sugar, beating between each addition.

Sift half of the confectioners' sugar into the bowl and gently fold it into the egg whites with a large metal spoon. Add the remaining confectioners' sugar and fold it in without overmixing and losing the air. The mixture should look glossy, smooth and light.

Ease a heaped tablespoonful of the meringue mixture onto the prepared baking sheet into a circle. Repeat with the remaining mixture to make 8 circles. Bake for 1 to 1¼ hours until the meringues are risen and sound hollow when tapped gently underneath. Leave the meringues to cool completely on a wire rack.

Line the bottom and sides of a 9- x 5-inch bread pan with a double layer of plastic wrap, leaving a generous overhang of wrap on all sides.

Beat the egg yolks and sugar in a large bowl until pale and fluffy. Fold in the lemon zest and curd. Whip the cream in a second bowl until it forms soft peaks, then gently fold the cream into the egg yolk mixture.

In a clean mixing bowl and using clean beaters, beat the egg whites until they will form stiff peaks. Gently fold them into the egg yolk mixture. Spoon half of the semifreddo mixture into the prepared bread pan. Break 2 of the meringues into fairly chunky pieces and scatter them over, then top with the remaining semifreddo mixture. Cover the top with the excess plastic wrap, then freeze for about 5 hours until firm.

Once firm, unmold the semifreddo onto a serving plate and remove the plastic wrap. Crumble 2 more of the meringues over the top and sprinkle with a little lemon zest. Serve cut into slices. Any leftovers can be returned to the freezer, double-wrapped in plastic wrap.

POACHED PEACHES IN LEMONGRASS & GINGER SYRUP

Peaches, nectarines, pears, plums and cherries, in fact any slightly firm fruit, can be poached. It's best to use just-ripe or even slightly underripe fruit, because if it is too soft there is a danger it will not hold its shape. Here, peaches are poached in a ginger- and lemongrass-infused syrup. You can replace half of the water with white rum or rosé wine.

**SERVES 4 PREPARATION TIME: 10 MINUTES, PLUS COOLING AND CHILLING
COOKING TIME: 25 MINUTES**

½ cup sugar
4 tablespoons honey
1 lemongrass stalk, outer layer removed
  and bruised with the blade of a knife

2-inch piece fresh gingerroot, peeled
  and sliced
juice of ½ lemon
6 just-ripe peaches, halved and pitted

To make the poaching liquid, put 2 cups water, the sugar, honey, lemongrass, ginger and lemon juice in a nonreactive saucepan. Bring to a boil, stirring to dissolve the sugar. Turn down the heat to low and simmer for 5 minutes.

Add the peaches and poach, turning them every so often, for 8 to 10 minutes until tender. Using a slotted spoon, remove the peaches and leave to one side until cool enough to handle.

Increase the heat under the pan and bring the poaching liquid to a boil, then let it bubble away until it reduces to about 1¼ cups light syrup. Leave to one side to cool, then remove and discard the lemongrass and ginger.

Carefully peel the peaches and put them in a serving bowl. Pour the syrup over the peaches and chill until ready to serve. They will keep for up to 2 days in the refrigerator.

Canning Poached Fruit

*Poached peaches and other fruit can be successfully canned for longer storage.
After poaching the fruit and lifting it out, don't let the syrup cool. Pack the fruit into sterilized canning jars, leaving headroom, and fill with boiling syrup so the fruit is submerged. Seal the jars, then process in a boiling-water bath (see pages 11 to 12)—the timing depends on the fruit's acidity levels and the size of the jar. Remove the jars and leave to cool.
Store in a cool, dry, dark place for up to 6 months.*

RHUBARB BRÛLÉES

Rhubarb and custard—is there a more delicious combination? The tartness of the fruit is perfect with sweet, creamy custard, which is best made up to a day in advance.

**SERVES 4   PREPARATION TIME: 15 MINUTES, PLUS CHILLING AND SETTING
COOKING TIME: 45 MINUTES**

1¼ cups heavy cream
1 vanilla bean, split lengthwise
4 extra-large egg yolks
2 tablespoons sugar, plus extra for
  sprinkling

RHUBARB COMPOTE:
1⅔ cups chopped rhubarb
2 tablespoons sugar
2 tablespoons orange juice

Heat the oven to 325°F. First make the rhubarb compote. Combine the rhubarb, sugar and orange juice in a nonmetallic pan. Bring to a boil, stirring to dissolve the sugar, then turn down the heat and simmer for 10 to 12 minutes until the rhubarb is tender and broken down. Remove the pan from the heat and leave the rhubarb to cool.

Heat the cream in another small pan with the vanilla bean until it almost comes to a boil.

Meanwhile, beat the egg yolks with the sugar until pale. Beat in the hot cream. Strain the custard into a measuring jug. (Rinse the vanilla bean, dry well and insert into a jar of sugar to make vanilla sugar.)

Spoon the rhubarb into four ⅔-cup ramekins. Pour the custard over the rhubarb until almost to the top of each ramekin. Put the ramekins in a roasting pan and pour in enough just-boiled water to come halfway up the sides. Bake for 20 to 25 minutes until the top of each custard is just set. Remove ramekins from the oven and leave to cool. Cover with plastic wrap and chill overnight (or a minimum of 2 hours, if you can't wait).

Heat the broiler. Sprinkle a thin layer of sugar over each custard and place under the broiler, close to the heat, until the sugar bubbles and starts to caramelize. Or use a blowtorch. Take care either way, because the sugar can easily burn. Leave the sugar to harden and cool slightly, then serve immediately.

Fruit Compotes

Delicious for breakfast when mixed with thick plain yogurt or as a simple dessert, fruit compotes are made of whole or pieces of fruit that are cooked in a sugar syrup until they become soft and take on a sticky sweetness. The fruit syrup can be flavored with vanilla, cinnamon, cloves or strips of orange or lemon zest, among many other ingredients.

Pineapple in Vanilla Rum

Preserving fruit in alcohol is one of the oldest and most delicious ways to extend the life of fresh fruit. It's worth experimenting with different types of fruit and alcohol—clementines in brandy, raspberries in vodka, figs in red wine—the options are endless.

**MAKES 4 CUPS   PREPARATION TIME: 10 MINUTES
COOKING TIME: 20 MINUTES, PLUS COOLING AND 1 MONTH INFUSING**

1 large, just-ripe pineapple
1½ cups sugar
1 cinnamon stick
1 vanilla bean
1 cup plus 2 tablespoons white rum

Stand the pineapple upright on a cutting board. Cut away the green top, the tough outer skin and the "eyes," then remove the core with a corer, if you have one. Alternatively remove the core after the pineapple is sliced. Cut the pineapple into slices, then cut each slice into quarters.

Put ¾ cup water and half the sugar into a large, wide, shallow saucepan. Add the cinnamon and vanilla and simmer over low heat, stirring until the sugar dissolves.

Add the pineapple to the sugar syrup and simmer over low heat for 5 minutes, turning the fruit once.

Put a colander over a bowl and spoon the pineapple into it. Return any of the syrup that has dripped into the bowl to the pan and leave the pineapple to cool.

Add the remaining sugar to the poaching liquid and simmer, stirring until the sugar dissolves. Increase the heat and bring to a boil. Continue to boil the liquid until the temperature rises to 230°F on a candy thermometer and it is syrupy. Carefully pour the syrup into a large measuring jug and leave to cool. Stir the rum into the cool syrup until combined.

Spoon the cooled pineapple into a sterilized jar along with the vanilla bean; discard the cinnamon stick. Pour the rum syrup over to cover the fruit completely. Cover the jar with a lid and store in a cool, dry, dark place for 1 month before using. It will keep for up to 6 months, but keep in the refrigerator once opened and use within 1 month.

COCONUT & LIME BAKED CHEESECAKE WITH **PINEAPPLE IN VANILLA RUM**

There is nothing quite like a classic baked cheesecake, and while it is delicious served plain, this version topped with whipped vanilla cream and rum-soaked pineapple is sublime.

**SERVES 8 TO 10   PREPARATION TIME: 25 MINUTES, PLUS COOLING
COOKING TIME: 1 HOUR 20 MINUTES**

butter, for greasing
1 cup plus 2 tablespoons ricotta cheese
1¾ cups farmer's cheese or cream cheese
2 teaspoons vanilla extract
finely grated zest and juice of 1 lime
3 eggs
¾ cup plus 2 tablespoons sugar

CRUST:
3 tablespoons unsweetened shredded
   coconut
18 gingersnap cookies, crushed
5 tablespoons unsalted butter, melted

TOPPING:
1 cup plus 2 tablespoons whipping cream
1 teaspoon vanilla extract
1 tablespoon confectioners' sugar
⅓ recipe quantity Pineapple
   in Vanilla Rum (see facing page),
   well drained
ground ginger and the pared zest
   of 1 lime, cut into fine strips, to serve

Heat the oven to 300°F. Grease the side of a deep 8-inch springform cake pan with butter and line the bottom with parchment paper. Lightly butter the paper.

To make the cheesecake crust, put the coconut in a large, nonstick skillet and toast, stirring occasionally, over medium-low heat for 3 minutes, or until light golden. Put the coconut in a large bowl and leave to cool.

When the coconut is cool, add the crushed cookies and melted butter and stir until combined. Tip the mixture into the prepared pan and press down with the back of a spoon into a firm, even layer. Leave to cool completely, then cover with plastic wrap and chill until needed.

Put the ricotta, farmer's cheese and vanilla in a blender and blend until smooth, then add the lime zest and juice, eggs and sugar and blend again until combined.

Pour the cheese mixture over the gingersnap crust and bake for 1¼ hours, or until set, but still a little wobbly. Remove the cheesecake from the oven and leave to cool in the pan on a wire rack.

To make the topping, using a hand-held electric mixer, whip the cream with the vanilla and confectioners' sugar until it will form soft peaks. Transfer the cheesecake to a serving plate and spoon the whipped cream over the top. Pile the pineapple on the cream and sprinkle with a little ground ginger and lime zest before serving.

CHOCOLATE RISOTTO WITH BOOZY CHERRIES

A sweet risotto might sound unusual, but the short-grain Arborio rice is equally happy used in a rice pudding as it is in a savory risotto. Serve this intensely chocolatey pudding in small bowls, topped with the cherries steeped in kirsch and a splash of light cream, if you like.

SERVES 4 TO 6 PREPARATION TIME: 15 MINUTES, PLUS RESTING
COOKING TIME: 50 MINUTES

3¾ cups whole milk
¼ cup sugar
¾ cup Arborio rice
2¼ ounces dark chocolate, about 70% cocoa solids, cut into small pieces
1 teaspoon vanilla bean paste
light cream, to serve (optional)

BOOZY CHERRIES:
1½ pounds dark cherries
¼ cup sugar
3 tablespoons kirsch or brandy
2 teaspoons cornstarch

Heat the oven to 300°F. Put the milk, sugar and rice in a Dutch oven. Bring the milk almost to a boil, stirring occasionally with a wooden spoon. Add the chocolate and keep stirring until it melts.

Stir in the vanilla, cover and transfer to the oven. Bake for 40 to 45 minutes, stirring occasionally, until the rice is tender. Stir any skin that forms on the surface into the rice, then leave it to rest, covered, for 5 minutes before serving.

Meanwhile, make the boozy cherries. Put the cherries, sugar and 2 tablespoons water in a saucepan and bring to a simmer, stirring until the sugar dissolves. Mix together the kirsch and cornstarch, then gradually stir this mixture into the cherries. Simmer for 2 to 3 minutes longer, until the sauce is thick and the cherries are tender.

Serve the chocolate risotto topped with the cherries and a swirl of cream, if you like. Any leftover boozy cherries can be stored for up to 1 week in the refrigerator.

Preserving Fruit in Alcohol

Steeping in alcohol is one of the easiest ways to preserve fruit. To make a longer-lasting version of Boozy Cherries, follow the instructions on page 182 for Pineapple in Vanilla Rum, using the same quantity of cherries as above, 1½ cups sugar and 1 cup plus 2 tablespoons kirsch or brandy. You can also flavor the sugar syrup with 2 star anise. The cherries will keep for up to 6 months stored in a cool, dry, dark place. Once opened, keep in the refrigerator and use within 1 month.

EXOTIC PLUM PUDDING WITH COCONUT & RUM CREAM

The traditional British Christmas plum pudding is given a tropical twist with the addition of dried mango, spices and dark rum. Don't be put off by the long list of ingredients, because this is easy to make. To make the pudding in advance, leave it to cool after steaming, then cover with fresh wax paper and foil. Store in a cool, dark place for up to 2 months. To reheat, steam the pudding for 2 hours, following the directions below.

SERVES 6   PREPARATION TIME: 30 MINUTES, PLUS SOAKING   COOKING TIME: 3 HOURS

5 ounces dried mango
⅔ cup all-purpose flour
4 teaspoons unsweetened cocoa powder
2 cups fresh white bread crumbs
1 teaspoon apple pie spice
1 teaspoon ground cinnamon
1 teaspoon ground ginger
¾ cup packed dark brown sugar
⅔ cup chilled butter, diced, plus extra for greasing
1 cup chopped pitted dates
1¼ cups raisins

3 ounces dark chocolate, about 70% cocoa solids, chopped
grated zest of 1 large orange
3 eggs, lightly beaten
5 tablespoons dark rum, plus extra to serve

COCONUT AND RUM CREAM:
1 cup heavy cream
½ cup coconut cream
4 tablespoons dark rum
3 tablespoons confectioners' sugar, or to taste

Put the mango in a bowl, cover with hot water and leave to soften for 1 hour. Drain well, then roughly chop the mango and leave to one side. Lightly grease a 5-cup pudding bowl or other heatproof bowl.

Sift the flour and cocoa powder into a large bowl, then stir in the bread crumbs, ground spices and sugar. Cut the butter into the mixture until it resembles coarse bread crumbs. Stir in the chopped mango, dates, raisins, chocolate and orange zest.

Mix together the eggs and dark rum, then pour over the fruit mixture and stir until combined. Spoon the mixture into the prepared bowl to ½ inch below the rim. Gently tap the bowl on the countertop to release any air bubbles and smooth the top with the back of a spoon.

Cover the pudding with a circle of wax paper and a double layer of foil, each with a pleat down the middle so the pudding can expand, then secure with string. Set the pudding on an upturned saucer or rack in a large saucepan. Pour in enough boiling water to come halfway up the side of the bowl. Cover the pan and steam for 3 hours, or until cooked and firm. Replenish the water during the steaming, as necessary.

To make the coconut and rum cream, whip the heavy cream and coconut cream together in a bowl, then fold in the rum and sugar, adding more to taste. Spoon the cream into a serving bowl and chill. Unmold the pudding onto a serving plate. Pour a little rum over and set alight. Serve with the coconut and rum cream.

RASPBERRY, AMARETTI & SALTED CARAMEL VERRINES

A verrine is a layered dessert that works best visually and flavor-wise when there are contrasting layers of color and texture. The combination of crisp crunch from the amaretti cookies; sticky, salty caramel sauce; thick whipped cream; and slightly tart raspberries make these verrines a great success.

SERVES 4   PREPARATION TIME: 20 MINUTES   COOKING TIME: 8 MINUTES

1¾ cups plus 2 tablespoons heavy cream
1 teaspoon vanilla bean paste
4 teaspoons confectioners' sugar
16 amaretti cookies, roughly crumbled
1½ cups raspberries

SALTED CARAMEL SAUCE:
6 tablespoons unsalted butter
1 unpacked cup light brown sugar
½ teaspoon vanilla bean paste
½ cup heavy cream
¼ teaspoon sea salt flakes

First make the salted caramel sauce. Melt the butter in a small saucepan over medium-low heat. Add the sugar and stir until it dissolves. Add the vanilla and cream and bring to boiling point. Turn down the heat and simmer, stirring, for 5 minutes, or until thicker and the color of toffee. Stir in the salt and leave to one side.

Using a hand-held electric mixer, whip the cream until it starts to become thick. Add the vanilla and sugar and continue to whip until soft peaks will form.

Crumble one-quarter of the amaretti into each glass. Top with a layer of the salted caramel sauce, followed by a layer of whipped cream topped off with raspberries. Chill until ready to serve.

F. Baked Goods

OATCAKES

Perfect to serve with your favorite cheese, smoked salmon or a selection of cold cuts, these Scottish savory crackers are traditionally plain, but you can experiment with different flavorings. For herb oatcakes, stir in ½ to 1 teaspoon thyme, rosemary, sage or parsley. Adding spices, such as cayenne pepper, smoked paprika and celery salt, are other good savory options. For sweet oatcakes, add apple pie spice, sugar or finely chopped dried fruit to the dry ingredients. Shredded sharp cheddar cheese or sesame seeds are also good additions.

MAKES 16   PREPARATION TIME: 10 MINUTES   COOKING TIME: 18 MINUTES

⅔ cup whole spelt flour
   or ½ cup all-purpose flour, plus extra
   for dusting
1 teaspoon baking soda

½ teaspoon salt
scant 1 cup medium steel-cut oats,
   plus extra for dusting
4 tablespoons unsalted butter

Heat the oven to 350°F and line a baking sheet with parchment paper.

Sift the flour, baking soda and salt into a mixing bowl, then stir in the oats. Cut in the butter until the mixture resembles coarse bread crumbs. Stir in about 3 tablespoons water and bring the mixture together to make a dough. Lightly knead the dough in the bowl to make a ball.

Lightly dust the countertop with a mixture of flour and oats. Roll out the dough on the countertop until about ⅛ inch thick and use a 2¼-inch fluted, round cookie cutter to cut out 16 circles. Put on the prepared baking sheet and bake for 15 to 18 minutes until crisp. Leave the oatcakes to cool on a wire rack, then store in an airtight container for up to 3 days.

Steel-Cut Oats

Steel-cut oats, also called Scotch oats, are made from cutting or grinding whole oats (groats) and are available in various grades. For these oatcakes, the medium-grade oats give a slightly coarse texture and nutty flavor. If you prefer a finer- or coarser-textured oatcake, feel free to adapt the oats you use. Bear in mind, however, that a dough made with coarse oats is difficult to work with because it is crumbly.

CHEESE & CAYENNE CRACKERS

These light, crumbly, cheese-flavored crackers are always popular with my friends. They make the perfect nibble with drinks or a delicious savory snack topped with a spoonful of a mild soft goat cheese and a piece of sun-blush tomato.

MAKES 20   PREPARATION TIME: 15 MINUTES, PLUS CHILLING   COOKING TIME: 15 MINUTES

1⅓ cups all-purpose flour, sifted, plus
   extra for dusting
1 teaspoon cayenne pepper

5 tablespoons butter, diced
¾ cup shredded sharp cheddar cheese

Put the flour and half of the cayenne into a mixing bowl. Cut in the butter to make a soft, slightly crumbly mixture, then stir in the cheddar cheese. Form into a soft ball of dough and knead briefly in the bowl until the cheese is evenly distributed. Wrap the dough in plastic wrap and chill for 30 minutes to firm up.

Line a large baking sheet with parchment paper. Roll out the dough on a lightly floured countertop into a long rectangle about 2¾ inches wide and ¼ inch thick. Cut into 1-inch-wide fingers and arrange, spaced apart, on the baking sheet. Chill for another 20 minutes to firm up. This help the crackers keep their shape during baking.

Meanwhile, heat the oven to 375°F. Sprinkle the crackers with the remaining cayenne and bake for 12 to 15 minutes until golden and crisp. Leave the crackers to cool on a wire rack, then store in an airtight container for up to 3 days.

"SLEEPLESS" SPELT BREAD

This bread uses an overnight starter—hence the name—that not only improves the flavor, but gives it a good crust and extends its keeping qualities. I've used whole spelt flour in this recipe, but you can use regular bread flour, if preferred.

MAKES 2 LOAVES   PREPARATION TIME: 20 MINUTES, PLUS OVERNIGHT RISING AND A SECOND RISING   COOKING TIME: 30 MINUTES

10 cups whole spelt flour, plus extra
   for dusting
½ envelope (¼-oz.) instant active dry
   yeast
heaped 1 tablespoon sea salt

vegetable oil, for greasing
1 egg, lightly beaten
1 tablespoon oatmeal, for sprinkling
   (optional)

The day before you intend to bake, mix together the flour, yeast and salt in a large mixing bowl. Using a fork and then your fingers, slowly mix in 2½ cups lukewarm (120° to 130°F) water, using enough to make a soft dough.

Knead the dough on a lightly floured countertop for 10 minutes, or until it is smooth and elastic. Shape the dough into a ball. Wash, dry and lightly grease the bowl. Put the dough in the bowl and cover with plastic wrap. Leave to rise at room temperature overnight, or for about 9 hours, or until it doubles in volume. (The dough can be left for up to 16 hours, if necessary.)

The next day, punch down the dough by pressing it with your knuckles, then tip it out of the bowl onto a lightly floured countertop. Divide the dough into 2 equal portions and shape each into a ball. Put the loaves on a floured cookie sheet, cover with a clean dish towel and leave to rise again at room temperature for 2 to 3 hours until almost doubled in size.

Meanwhile, heat the oven to 425°F. Brush the top of each loaf with beaten egg and scatter the oatmeal over, if using. Bake for 25 to 30 minutes until golden brown and hollow sounding when tapped underneath. Leave the loaves to cool on wire racks.

Spelt Flour

Once widely grown in parts of Europe, spelt is undergoing a revival due in part to its traditional "what wheat used to taste like" flavor and the fact that it can usually be eaten by those with a wheat intolerance. This ancient variety of wheat produces a pale, grayish flour and has a slightly nutty flavor. It is used to make bread, as well as piecrusts, crackers and cakes.

SOURDOUGH

Sourdough bread has become hugely popular, but the origins of this artisan, long-fermented, natural yeast bread go way back. If you haven't made sourdough before, it's a labor of love and requires time and patience, but it's hugely rewarding when you produce a magnificent airy-textured, golden, crusty loaf—and it can become slightly addictive!

**MAKES 1 LOAF   PREPARATION TIME: STARTER 5 DAYS; SPONGE 5 MINUTES
PLUS OVERNIGHT STANDING; LOAF 25 MINUTES, PLUS 2 RISINGS
COOKING TIME: 40 MINUTES**

STARTER:
2½ cups white bread flour (used in five
    ½-cup portions)

SPONGE STARTER:
1¼ cups starter (see above; keep the
    remaining starter for your next batch
    of bread. Put it in a canning jar,
    cover and keep in the refrigerator
    until needed.)
2 cups organic white bread flour

DOUGH:
2 cups white bread flour, plus extra
    for dusting
1 tablespoon honey
1 tablespoon sea salt
vegetable oil, for greasing

TO MAKE THE STARTER:

Day 1
Put 4 tablespoons filtered room-temperature water and ½ cup of the white bread flour in a large canning jar. Stir well until combined, then cover with a clean dish towel. Leave at room temperature for 24 hours.

Day 2
Add another 4 tablespoons filtered room-temperature water and another ½ cup of the flour to the canning jar. Stir well until combined, then cover with a clean dish towel. Leave at room temperature for 24 hours.

Day 3
Repeat Day 2.

Day 4
Repeat Day 2.

Day 5
Repeat Day 2.

Day 6
The starter is now ready to use. You should have a lively, bubbly starter the consistency of thick paint, and it should smell like beer, sweet and slightly yeasty. This will develop with use and age.

TO MAKE THE SPONGE STARTER:

Transfer 1¼ cups of the starter to a large mixing bowl and add 1¼ cups filtered room-temperature water and the 2 cups organic white bread flour. Mix until combined. Cover with plastic wrap and leave overnight at room temperature. The mixture will increase in volume and will look puffy and bubbly.

TO MAKE THE DOUGH:

Add the flour, honey and salt to the sponge starter. Mix well, then cover with plastic wrap and leave for 20 minutes. Tip out onto a floured countertop and knead for 10 to 15 minutes. The dough will be very soft and sticky at first, but keep kneading until it becomes a smooth, elastic ball of dough. (If the dough is unmanageably wet before kneading, add extra flour; alternatively, if it is too dry, add a splash more water.)

Put the dough in a lightly greased bowl. Cover with lightly greased plastic wrap and leave at room temperature for about 8 hours or overnight, or until it doubles in volume. Tip out the dough onto a lightly floured countertop and fold the ends into the middle. Repeat the folding a second time.

Shape the dough into a round loaf and put it into a colander lined with a clean dish towel liberally dusted with flour, or a floured bread-rising basket. Cover with lightly greased plastic wrap and leave to rise for about 3 hours until almost doubled in size. Gently tip out the dough onto a lightly greased and floured cookie sheet. Dust the top of the loaf with flour and slash a few times with a sharp knife. Leave to rise, uncovered, at room temperature for 1 hour.

Heat the oven to 450°F. Just before you put the loaf in the oven, put a roasting pan half-filled with just-boiled water in the bottom of the oven. (This creates a steamy atmosphere in the oven to make a loaf with a good rise and crust.) Put the loaf in the oven and bake for 20 minutes, then reduce the oven temperature to 400°F and bake for 20 minutes longer, or until risen and hollow sounding when tapped underneath. Transfer to a wire rack to cool. Enjoy!

Sourdough Starter

Instead of commercial yeast, a sourdough loaf is made with a fermented batterlike starter, which uses yeasts found naturally in the atmosphere and in the flour. A starter is made with a combination of flour and water (filtered is best). I've used white bread flour but you could use rye or spelt instead. It initially needs six days to get going, but it will become more active with time—it keeps for years!

To keep a starter "alive," feed it every 4 days with 3 tablespoons white bread flour and 3 tablespoons room-temperature filtered water. Stir, then cover and keep it in the refrigerator. Ideally, also feed your starter the day before you intend to bake. If you do not bake sourdough bread regularly, you can end up with too much starter, in which case discard some of it (or use to make a pizza crust) and continue feeding as instructed above. It might develop a layer of slightly gray liquid on top but this is normal. Just be sure to stir the starter before you use it.

PROVENÇAL FOUGASSE

This leaf-shaped flatbread is the French version of focaccia. Once traditionally made for Christmas in Provence, fougasse is now eaten all year around and can be both sweet and savory, or, indeed, made without any extra flavorings.

**MAKES 2 LOAVES   PREPARATION TIME: 30 MINUTES, PLUS 2 RISINGS
COOKING TIME: 35 MINUTES**

2 teaspoons active dry yeast
4 cups white bread flour
2 teaspoons salt
5 tablespoons olive oil, plus extra for
  greasing and drizzling

4 teaspoons Provençal mixed dried herbs
4 garlic cloves, sliced
12 cherry tomatoes, halved
sea salt flakes

Put 6 tablespoons lukewarm (105° to 115°F) water into a bowl and sprinkle the yeast over the top. Stir, then leave for 5 minutes, or until the yeast dissolves and is slightly frothy. Meanwhile, line two large cookie sheets with parchment paper and leave to one side.

Put the flour and salt into a large mixing bowl and stir until combined, then make a well in the middle. Pour the yeast mixture, oil, herbs and an additional ¾ cup lukewarm water into the well. Gradually draw in the flour with your hand. Add extra water, 1 tablespoon at a time if necessary, to make a soft, but not too sticky, dough.

Tip the dough onto a lightly floured countertop and knead for 10 minutes, or until it forms a smooth, elastic ball of dough. Wash, dry and lightly grease the bowl. Return the dough to the bowl, cover with a clean dish towel and leave for 2 hours, or until doubled in volume.

Punch down the dough by pressing with your knuckles, then tip it onto a lightly floured countertop. Divide the dough into 2 equal pieces and leave to rest for 15 minutes, covered with the dish towel. On the lightly floured surface, use the palm of your hands to flatten each piece into an oval about ¾ inch thick.

Using a small, sharp knife, make evenly spaced diagonal cuts through the dough, making sure you do not cut through the sides or the bottom. Very gently lift the loaf slightly and carefully stretch it to open up the cuts a little. Transfer the flatbreads to the cookie sheets. Cover with plastic wrap or the dish towel and leave to rise for about 30 minutes until almost doubled in thickness.

Meanwhile, heat the oven to 375°F. Press the garlic into the shaped dough and top with the tomatoes. Drizzle olive oil over the tops and sprinkle sea salt flakes over both. Bake for 30 to 35 minutes until golden and hollow sounding when tapped underneath. Transfer the loaves to wire racks to cool. Eat while warm or at room temperature.

RED ONION & GRUYÈRE FOCACCIA

This light Italian bread is enriched with olive oil, and in this recipe is topped with red onion, Gruyère cheese and sprigs of thyme. It can also be made simply with a sprinkling of sea salt flakes and a drizzle of extra virgin olive oil.

MAKES 1 LOAF   PREPARATION TIME: 10 MINUTES PLUS OVERNIGHT STANDING; DOUGH 35 MINUTES, PLUS 2 RISINGS   COOKING TIME: 40 MINUTES

STARTER:
½ teaspoon active dry yeast
1 cup white bread flour

DOUGH:
1 teaspoon active dry yeast
3 cups white bread flour, plus extra
   for dusting
2 teaspoons salt
3 tablespoons olive oil, plus extra
   for greasing
1 tablespoon honey

TOPPING:
2 red onions, each cut into 8 wedges
1 cup grated Gruyère cheese
6 long thyme sprigs
3 tablespoons extra virgin olive oil
½ teaspoon sea salt flakes

To make the starter, sprinkle the yeast into ⅔ cup lukewarm (105° to 115°F) water in a large bowl. Stir, then leave for 5 minutes, or until the yeast dissolves and is slightly frothy. Add the flour and mix to form a thick batter. Cover with a clean dish towel and leave at room temperature overnight, or up to 24 hours, or until it becomes a loose, bubbling batter.

To make the dough, sprinkle the yeast into ⅔ cup lukewarm water. Stir, then leave for 5 minutes, or until the yeast dissolves and is slightly frothy. Mix the flour and salt together in a large mixing bowl. Make a well in the middle and pour in the starter, the yeasted water, olive oil and honey. Gradually draw in the flour with your hand. Add extra water, 1 tablespoon at a time, if needed, to make a soft, but not too sticky, dough.

Tip the dough onto a lightly floured countertop and knead for 10 minutes, or until it forms a smooth, elastic ball of dough. Wash, dry and lightly grease the bowl. Return the dough to the bowl, cover with a clean dish towel and leave for 2 hours, or until doubled in volume. Lightly grease a cookie sheet and leave to one side.

Punch down the dough by pressing with your knuckles, then tip it out onto a lightly floured countertop. Leave it to rest for 15 minutes, covered with the dish towel. Roll out the dough into a circle until about 9 inches in diameter. Put the dough on the cookie sheet and cover with a dish towel. Leave to rise for 40 minutes, or until almost doubled in size. Meanwhile, heat the oven to 400°F.

To make the topping, press the dough with your fingertips to make indents about ½ inch deep. Scatter the onions over in an even layer, then sprinkle with the Gruyère, thyme, oil and sea salt. Bake the focaccia for 30 to 40 minutes until risen and hollow sounding when tapped underneath. Leave to cool a little on a wire rack and serve cut into wedges.

CRANBERRY & PISTACHIO BISCOTTI

Delicious dipped into a glass of Vin Santo, Italian dessert wine, or a cup of espresso, these double-baked Italian cookies keep for up to three months in an airtight container. You can use chopped dried apricots, figs or sour cherries in place of the cranberries, if preferred.

MAKES ABOUT 28   PREPARATION TIME: 20 MINUTES, PLUS COOLING
COOKING TIME: 1 HOUR

scant 2½ cups all-purpose flour,
   plus extra for dusting
1 teaspoon baking powder
1 teaspoon ground cinnamon
¾ cup plus 3 tablespoons sugar
3 eggs, lightly beaten

2 teaspoons vanilla bean paste
⅔ cup dried cranberries
⅔ cup unsalted shelled pistachios, halved,
   or a mixture of pistachios and blanched
   almonds

Heat the oven to 350°F and line two cookie sheets with parchment paper.

Sift the flour, baking powder and cinnamon into a mixing bowl and stir in the sugar. Add the eggs and vanilla and mix to a soft dough. Stir in the cranberries and pistachios.

Turn out the dough onto a lightly floured countertop and knead lightly into a ball. Divide the dough into two equal portions and roll each half into a 1¼-inch-thick log. Put on one of the prepared cookie sheets, about 2 inches apart, because they spread slightly. Bake for 30 minutes, or until firm and light golden. Leave to cool for 10 minutes and reduce the oven temperature to 300°F.

Using a serrated knife, cut the biscotti on the diagonal into ½-inch-thick slices. Lay the biscotti flat on the cookie sheets and return to the oven for 15 minutes. Turn the biscotti over and bake for 10 to 15 minutes longer until golden and crisp. Leave to cool on a wire rack and store in an airtight container.

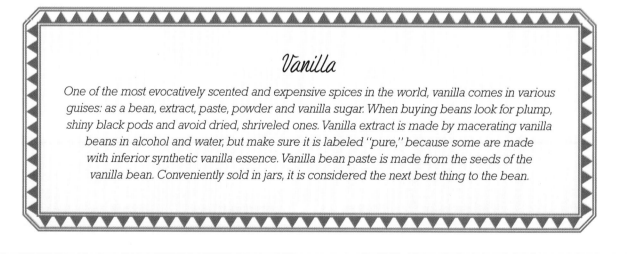

Vanilla

One of the most evocatively scented and expensive spices in the world, vanilla comes in various guises: as a bean, extract, paste, powder and vanilla sugar. When buying beans look for plump, shiny black pods and avoid dried, shriveled ones. Vanilla extract is made by macerating vanilla beans in alcohol and water, but make sure it is labeled "pure," because some are made with inferior synthetic vanilla essence. Vanilla bean paste is made from the seeds of the vanilla bean. Conveniently sold in jars, it is considered the next best thing to the bean.

GINGER & CHOCOLATE SHORTBREAD

These cookies are buttery and crumbly with a slight heat from the preserved ginger and delicious pools of melted chocolate—irresistible!

**MAKES 10   PREPARATION TIME: 20 MINUTES, PLUS CHILLING AND COOLING
COOKING TIME: 30 MINUTES**

1¾ sticks (14 tablespoons) unsalted
butter, softened, plus extra for greasing
½ cup confectioners' sugar
1 teaspoon vanilla bean paste
a pinch salt
1⅔ cups all-purpose flour, sifted
⅔ cup rice flour or ¾ cup cornstarch,
sifted

2½ ounces dark chocolate, about
70% cocoa solids, chopped,
or scant ⅓ cup chocolate chips
4 tablespoons chopped preserved ginger
in syrup, drained
granulated sugar, for dusting

Heat the oven to 350°F and lightly grease an 8-inch fluted, loose-bottomed tart pan with butter.

Using a hand-held electric mixer, cream the butter and confectioners' sugar until pale and fluffy, then beat in the vanilla, salt, all-purpose flour and rice flour. Add the chocolate and ginger and knead lightly until evenly spread throughout the dough.

Press the dough into the prepared pan in an even layer using the back of a spoon, then chill for 30 minutes, or until firm.

Score the dough into 10 wedges and bake for 25 to 30 minutes until light golden and crisp. Remove the shortbread from the oven, put the pan on a wire rack and leave to cool for 10 minutes. Dust with granulated sugar, cut into wedges and leave to cool completely in the pan. Remove the shortbread from the pan and store in an airtight container.

ORANGE & ALMOND CAKE WITH HONEY SYRUP

Reminiscent of the classic Spanish Santiago cake, this light, moist cake has flecks of orange zest, which adds both flavor and color, and a sticky honey-syrup topping. Serve on its own or with a spoonful of whipped cream mixed with thick plain yogurt.

**SERVES 10 PREPARATION TIME: 20 MINUTES, PLUS COOLING
COOKING TIME: 1 HOUR 20 MINUTES**

1 large orange, about 9 ounces, roughly chopped including skin
3 tablespoons plus 1 teaspoon unsalted butter, melted, plus extra for greasing
5 eggs, at room temperature, separated
¾ cup plus 2 tablespoons sugar
1⅓ cups very finely ground blanched almonds

scant ½ cup all-purpose flour
2 tablespoons toasted slivered almonds and confectioners' sugar, to decorate

HONEY-SYRUP TOPPING:
juice of 1 large orange
3 tablespoons honey

Put the orange in a nonreactive pan with 4 tablespoons water. Cover with a lid and simmer the orange, stirring occasionally to prevent it from sticking, over very low heat for 30 minutes, or until the skin is soft and the liquid evaporates. Transfer the orange to a food processor or blender and finely chop. Alternatively, you can use a knife. Leave the orange to cool.

Heat the oven to 350°F and grease a deep 8-inch springform cake pan with butter. Line the bottom of the pan with a circle of parchment paper, cut to fit, and butter the paper.

Put the egg whites in a large, greasefree bowl and beat until they form stiff peaks. Gradually beat in half the sugar and continue beating for 1 minute, or until glossy.

In a second bowl, beat the eggs yolks with the remaining sugar for 2 minutes, or until pale, thick and creamy. Fold in the orange and melted butter, followed by the ground almonds and flour.

Gently stir in one-quarter of the egg whites to loosen the mixture, then, using a large metal spoon, gently fold in the remaining egg whites. Spoon the batter into the prepared pan and smooth the top. Bake for 50 minutes, or until risen and golden and a skewer inserted into the middle comes out clean. If the cake is browning too quickly, cover it loosely with foil.

Meanwhile, make the syrup. Strain the orange juice into a small pan and stir in the honey. Bring the mixture to a boil and let bubble away for 10 minutes, or until it reduces by half and is syrupy.

While the cake is still in the pan, pierce it all over with a skewer. Spoon the syrup over the cake, letting it seep into the holes. Leave the cake to cool for 10 minutes in the pan on a wire rack. Run a round-bladed knife around the inside edge of the pan to loosen the cake, then remove from the pan and peel off the paper. Leave to cool completely on the wire rack. Scatter the toasted almonds over and dust with confectioners' sugar before serving.

SOUR CHERRY & PECAN CHOCOLATE BROWNIE CAKE

This is a dense, rich cake with a moist inside and slightly crisp exterior. The cake rises and might crack slightly after baking, but this is all part of its charm.

**MAKE ABOUT 10 SLICES   PREPARATION TIME: 20 MINUTES, PLUS SOAKING
COOKING TIME: 50 MINUTES**

½ cup dried sour cherries
3 tablespoons brandy
1 stick (½ cup) unsalted butter, plus extra
  for greasing
8 ounces dark chocolate, about 70%
  cocoa solids, broken into pieces
1 cup plus 2 tablespoons sugar

4 extra-large eggs, separated
4 tablespoons all-purpose flour
½ cup shelled pecans,
  toasted and chopped
unsweetened cocoa powder, for dusting
whipped cream and fresh raspberries,
  to serve (optional)

Soak the cherries in the brandy for 30 minutes.

Heat the oven to 375°F and lightly grease a deep 8-inch springform cake pan with butter.

Melt the butter and chocolate in a heatproof bowl placed over a pan of gently simmering water, stirring occasionally. Make sure the bottom of the bowl does not touch the water. Carefully remove the bowl from the heat and leave the mixture to cool for a couple of minutes.

Stir the sugar into the melted chocolate, then beat in the egg yolks, one at a time, followed by the cherries and brandy and then the flour. Stir in the toasted pecans.

Using a hand-held electric mixer, beat the egg whites in a large, greasefree bowl until they form stiff peaks. Gently stir one-quarter of the egg whites into the batter to loosen it, then, using a large metal spoon, gently fold in the remaining egg whites in three batches.

Pour the batter into the prepared pan and smooth the top. Bake for 45 to 50 minutes until risen, but still slightly gooey in the middle. Leave the cake to cool for 10 minutes in the pan on a wire rack. Run a round-bladed knife around the inside edge of the pan to loosen the cake, then remove from the pan. Leave the cake to cool completely on the wire rack. Dust with cocoa powder before serving with whipped cream and raspberries, if you like.

Simple Raspberry & Apple Jam

This jam takes next to no time to make, which means the raspberries retain their fresh, fruity flavor and vibrant color. The addition of the pectin-rich apple helps the jam to set.

MAKES 2 X 7-OUNCE JARS   **PREPARATION TIME: 10 MINUTES**   **COOKING TIME: 20 MINUTES**

1 pint raspberries
1 teaspoon lemon juice
1 apple, about 5 ounces, peeled, cored and grated
1 cup plus 2 tablespoons sugar

Put the raspberries and lemon juice in a nonreactive pan over low heat and simmer until the juices begin to flow. Add the apple and sugar and stir until the sugar dissolves, then increase the heat and bring the mixture to a rapid, rolling boil. Boil for about 15 minutes, or until the jam is thick. Test for doneness with a jelly or candy thermometer (it should register 225°F). Or put a teaspoonful of the jam onto a cold saucer and let it cool for a few minutes, then push it with your finger. If the jam wrinkles, it is ready; if not, continue to boil for 2 minutes or so longer and retest.

If you prefer a smoother jam, press three-quarters of the mixture through a sterilized strainer to remove the seeds. Spoon the jam into sterilized jars and seal. Store in a dark, dry, cool place for up to 6 months. Once opened, keep in the refrigerator.

VANILLA & WHITE CHOCOLATE DRIZZLE CAKES WITH **RASPBERRY & APPLE JAM**

These individual cakes are a take on the classic sponge cake and are topped with a white chocolate glaze. Use a silicone muffin tray or a metal muffin pan.

MAKES 12   PREPARATION TIME: 30 MINUTES, PLUS COOLING   COOKING TIME: 20 MINUTES

1¾ cups unsalted butter, softened
1 cup sugar
1 teaspoon vanilla bean paste
4 eggs
1⅔ cups all-purpose flour, sifted
heaped 1 teaspoon baking powder
12 raspberries, to decorate

GLAZE:
4 tablespoons heavy cream
1½ ounces white chocolate, grated

FILLING:
¾ cup plus 2 tablespoons heavy cream
1 teaspoon vanilla bean paste
4 tablespoons Simple Raspberry & Apple Jam (see page 208)

Heat the oven to 350°F. If using a metal 12-cup muffin pan, line the cups with paper muffin or cupcake cases; a silicone muffin tray doesn't need to be lined. Using a hand-held electric mixer, cream the butter and sugar together until pale and fluffy. Add the vanilla and eggs, one at a time, beating in each before adding the next. Fold in the flour and baking powder.

Spoon the batter into the paper cases. Bake for 18 to 20 minutes until risen and light golden. Remove the pan from the oven and leave to cool on a wire rack for 5 minutes. Unmold the cakes onto a wire rack and leave to cool completely.

Meanwhile, make the glaze. Put the cream in a small saucepan and heat to boiling point. Remove the pan from the heat, add the white chocolate and stir until it melts. Leave the glaze to cool until it is thick enough to drizzle over the cakes.

To make the filling, whip the cream with the vanilla until it will form soft peaks.

To finish the cakes, slice each one in half horizontally. Spread 1 teaspoon of jam onto the bottom half and top with a heaped spoonful of whipped cream. Set the other half of the cake back in place. Drizzle the white chocolate glaze over each cake and top with a raspberry. Leave until the glaze sets before serving.

PANFORTE

Traditionally an Italian Christmas cake, this wonderfully sticky concoction of dark chocolate, nuts, dried fruit, spices and honey is so good that it's worth making at any time of the year.

MAKES 16 WEDGES   PREPARATION TIME: 20 MINUTES   COOKING TIME: 40 MINUTES

butter, for greasing
edible rice paper, for lining (optional)
1 cup shelled hazelnuts
heaped ¾ cup blanched almonds
½ cup all-purpose flour, sifted
1 tablespoon unsweetened cocoa powder
heaped 1 teaspoon apple pie spice
¾ cup chopped dried apricots

½ cup chopped dried figs
4 ounces dark chocolate, about
  70% cocoa solids, chopped
⅓ cup honey
⅓ cup granulated sugar
⅓ cup packed light brown sugar
confectioners' sugar, for dusting

Heat the oven to 350°F. Lightly grease an 8-inch springform cake pan with butter and line the bottom with parchment paper. For a more authentic appearance, line the bottom with a circle of edible rice paper.

Put the hazelnuts and almonds on two baking sheets and toast in the oven for about 9 minutes, turning once, until they start to color. Remove the nuts from the oven and leave them to cool, then chop them in half.

Sift the flour, cocoa powder and spice into a bowl, then stir in the dried apricots, figs and toasted nuts.

Put the chocolate, honey and granulated and brown sugars in a heavy-bottomed saucepan and warm over low heat, stirring until the chocolate melts. Pour the chocolate into the flour mixture and mix well to combine. Spoon the batter into the pan and, working quickly before it sets, spread into an even layer, first with the back of a spoon and then with your wet hands.

Bake for 25 to 30 minutes, or until just firm. Remove from the oven and leave to cool in the pan. When the panforte is cool, remove it from the pan, dust with confectioners' sugar and serve cut into wedges.

Dried Fruit

With its intense sweetness, dried fruit is an excellent alternative to sugar and comes with the bonus of being high in fiber. You can buy mixed bags, but for cooks who like to include dried fruit in their baking, or, indeed, in savory dishes, such as curries and tagines, the best option is to buy fruit separately so you can control the proportions. Always buy unsulfured apricots, which are deep orange in color and have a wonderful toffeelike taste.

SPICED BAKLAVA

Anyone with a sweet tooth will love this rich Middle Eastern treat. This version is made with layers of crisp phyllo pastry, filled with chopped nuts and sweetened with a lightly spiced rosewater syrup.

MAKES ABOUT 30 PIECES   PREPARATION TIME: 20 MINUTES   COOKING TIME: 1 HOUR

¾ cup unsalted butter, plus extra
  for greasing
20 phyllo pastry dough sheets, thawed
  if frozen
½ cup unsalted shelled pistachios,
  finely chopped
½ cup blanched almonds, finely chopped
finely grated zest of 1 orange
2 tablespoons sugar

SYRUP:
1½ cups sugar
juice of ½ lemon
6 cardamom pods, split
1 teaspoon ground cinnamon
2 tablespoons rosewater

Heat the oven to 325°F and lightly grease an 11- x 7-inch baking pan with butter.

Melt the butter in a saucepan over low heat. Cut the phyllo pastry dough to fit the pan, if necessary. Lay 10 sheets of the dough in the prepared pan, one sheet at a time and brushing with melted butter before adding the next sheet. Keep the remaining phyllo dough covered with a damp dish towel to prevent it from drying out.

Mix together the nuts, orange zest and sugar and spread the mixture over the dough in an even layer.

Layer the remaining phyllo on top of the nut mixture, brushing each sheet with butter as before. Using a sharp knife, cut a crisscross pattern into the top layers of dough to make a diamond pattern.

Bake for 45 minutes, or until the top is crisp and golden. Leave to one side to cool slightly.

Now make the syrup. Heat 1¼ cups water in a small pan with the sugar, lemon juice, cardamom and cinnamon, stirring until the sugar dissolves. Increase the heat and boil for 15 minutes, or until the liquid becomes syrupy. Stir in the rosewater, then remove the cardamom pods.

Using the cuts as a guide, cut the baklava into diamonds, then pour the syrup over the top, letting it soak into the cuts. Leave to cool completely before removing from the pan for serving.

FRENCH FRUIT TARTLETS

These stunning tartlets are filled with crème pâtissière and topped with fresh fruit—either choose a mixture of fruit in a range of colors or opt for a single variety. You can make the pastry cases and filling a day in advance, but assemble the tartlets just before serving. Instead of the crème pâtissière, a mixture of sweetened mascarpone and crème fraîche is equally delicious.

MAKES 8   PREPARATION TIME: 45 MINUTES, PLUS CHILLING   COOKING TIME: 25 MINUTES

PÂTE SUCRÉE:
2 cups all-purpose flour, sifted, plus extra
    for dusting
a pinch salt
7 tablespoons cold unsalted butter, cubed,
    plus extra for greasing
7 tablespoons sugar
1 egg, plus 2 egg yolks, lightly beaten

CRÈME PÂTISSIÈRE:
4 egg yolks
7 tablespoons plus 1½ teaspoons sugar

scant ½ cup all-purpose flour
1½ cups whole milk
1 vanilla bean, split lengthwise and
    seeds scraped out

TOPPING:
14 ounces mixed fruit, such as
    blueberries, blackberries,
    raspberries, strawberries and
    red and white currants, hulled
    and halved, if necessary
6 tablespoons red-currant jelly

To make the pâte sucrée, in a mixing bowl, rub together the flour, salt and butter using your fingertips. Stir in the sugar and add the whole egg and 2 egg yolks. Mix with a fork and then your fingers until the dough holds together, but don't overwork it or the pastry will be tough. (The pâte sucrée can also be made in a food processor.) Wrap the dough in plastic wrap, flatten into a disk and chill for at least 1 hour.

To make the crème pâtissière, put the egg yolks and sugar in a bowl. Using a hand-held electric mixer, beat for about 2 minutes until pale, thickened and creamy. Gradually fold in the flour. Heat the milk with the vanilla seeds to just below boiling point. Slowly pour the milk into the egg mixture, beating well. Return the mixture to the cleaned pan and bring to a boil, stirring to prevent lumps from forming. Turn down the heat and simmer for 3 minutes, stirring, until the mixture has the consistency of a thick custard. Spoon into a bowl and cover the surface with buttered parchment paper to prevent a skin from forming. Leave to cool completely, then refrigerate until required.

Lightly grease eight 3½-inch loose-bottomed tartlet pans with butter. Divide the dough into 8 equal pieces and roll out, one piece at a time, on a lightly floured countertop into a 4½-inch circle. Line the pans with the dough, trimming any excess. Chill for 30 minutes. (Alternatively, grease and line a 9-inch tart pan.)

Meanwhile, heat the oven to 400°F. Line each pastry shell with parchment paper, fill with baking beans and set on a cookie sheet. Bake for 10 minutes (25 minutes for a large tart). Remove the paper and beans and bake for 5 to 8 minutes longer until the pastry is golden and cooked. Leave to cool, then remove the pastry shells from the pans. Fill with the crème pâtissière and arrange the fruit on top. Gently heat the red-currant jelly with 1 tablespoon water, stirring until it melts. Leave to cool slightly, then brush the glaze over the fruit.

Rich Homemade Ricotta

Making ricotta is not as challenging as it might sound, and this version of the Italian soft cheese is wonderfully rich, creamy and indulgent. The taste will depend on the quality of the milk and the cream you use—the best-quality dairy products will obviously result in a ricotta with a superior flavor and texture.

**MAKES 1¾ CUPS   PREPARATION TIME: 10 MINUTES, PLUS STANDING
COOKING TIME: 15 MINUTES**

3¾ cups whole milk
½ cup heavy cream
½ teaspoon salt
3 tablespoons lemon juice

Heat the milk and cream with the salt in a large stainless-steel saucepan until the mixture reaches 190°F, stirring occasionally to prevent it catching on the bottom of the pan.

Remove the pan from the heat and add the lemon juice, then stir gently and slowly a few times. Leave for 5 minutes. The milk mixture should start to curdle and separate almost immediately.

Line a strainer with a large square of cheesecloth, folded into three layers, and set it over a bowl. Pour in the milk mixture and leave to drain for at least 1 hour. After 1 hour, you should have a spreadable cheese; after 2 hours, the ricotta will have the texture of soft cream cheese.

Discard the whey in the bowl and transfer the ricotta to a bowl if eating right away. Alternatively, transfer it to an airtight container and keep in the refrigerator for up to 3 days.

APPLE & HONEY TARTLETS WITH **RICOTTA**

Nothing beats the classic combination of honey-glazed apples and a buttery piecrust—unless, of course, there is a rich, sweet, vanilla-flavored ricotta cream too. Serve these warm.

MAKES 12   PREPARATION TIME: 30 MINUTES, PLUS CHILLING   COOKING TIME: 30 MINUTES

½ recipe quantity Rich Homemade
   Ricotta (see facing page)
1 teaspoon vanilla extract
⅓ cup sugar
2 eggs, separated
2 small, firm tart apples, peeled, cored
   and thinly sliced crosswise
2 tablespoons honey

PIECRUST:
1⅔ cups all-purpose flour, plus extra
   for dusting
a pinch salt
1 teaspoon sugar
½ cup cold unsalted butter, cubed,
   plus extra for greasing

To make the piecrust, sift the flour and salt into a mixing bowl, then stir in the sugar. Cut in the butter until the mixture resembles coarse bread crumbs. Drizzle in up to 2 tablespoons water, stirring with a fork and then your hands to bring the dough together into a ball. Wrap in plastic wrap and chill for at least 30 minutes.

Heat the oven to 375°. Lightly grease a 12-cup nonstick muffin pan. Roll out the dough on a lightly floured countertop, then cut out twelve 4-inch circles. Line the cups of the muffin pan with the dough so it reaches just above the edge of each one. Chill until ready to fill.

Mix together the ricotta, vanilla, sugar and egg yolks until smooth. Beat the egg whites until they will form stiff peaks. Gently fold the whites into the ricotta mixture. Spoon 2 heaped tablespoons into each tartlet shell and top with 3 or 4 apple slices. Bake for 30 minutes until the pastry is light golden and the filling has risen. Cool for 10 minutes, then unmold the tartlets onto a wire rack. Heat the honey and brush it over the apples.

INDEX

almonds
    Halloumi, Fig & Almond Salad 86
    Orange & Almond Cake with
        Honey Syrup 206
    Roasted Tomato Pesto 99
    Spiced Baklava 214
anchovies 8
    cured 47
    Fresh Marinated Anchovies 46
    Pissaladière with Marinated
        Anchovies 47
apples
    Apple & Honey Tartlets with
        Ricotta 219
    Cornish Blue, Bacon & Caramelized
        Apple Salad 77
    Sausages with Apple & Onion-Seed
        Chutney 35
    Simple Raspberry & Apple Jam
        208
    Slow-Cooked Pork with Apples
        & Cider Sauce 175
    Smoky Red-Pepper Ketchup 106
apricots
    Game, Chicken & Apricot Pie
        18–20
    Panforte 213
artichokes
    Artichoke & Oven-Roasted Tomato
        Confit 147
    Harissa & Tomato Couscous with
        Lemon-Roasted Vegetables 128
    Salad of Smoked Venison,
        Artichokes & Quail Eggs with
        Walnut Oil Dressing 105

bacon
    Bacon, Nectarine & Ginger Salad
        23
    Cornish Blue, Bacon & Caramelized
        Apple Salad 77
    Country-Style Pâté 27
    Home-Cured Bacon 22
    Pea, Bacon & Scamorza Frittatas
        137
    Tartiflette 91
Baklava, Spiced 214
basil
    Chimichurri Sauce 124
    Summer Herb Pesto 118
beans
    Cassoulet with Confit of Duck 33

Duck & Mango Salad with Citrus
    Dressing 104
Merguez Sausages & Smoked
    Paprika Beans 34
Piccalilli 138
beef
    Beef Carpaccio Salad with
        Thai Lemongrass & Chili Oil
        Dressing 109
    Beef, Porcini & Chestnut
        Bourguignon 152
    braising beef 42
    Pastrami with Sweet Cucumber
        Relish on Rye 21
    Steak & Ale Potpies 40–42
    Steak with Dolcelatte Sauce
        & Balsamic Tomatoes 92
    Tagliata with Chimichurri Sauce
        124
beets
    Beet Relish 71
    Ham Hock, Roasted Beets & Porcini
        Lentils 26
    Lamb, Beet & Puy Lentil Salad with
        Raspberry Vinegar Dressing 165
    Persian Lamb Chops with Eggplant
        Caviar & Beet Chips 151
    Piccalilli Rémoulade 139
bread
    Croutons 134
    Provençal Fougasse 201
    Red Onion & Gruyère Focaccia 202
    Skorthalia 115
    "Sleepless" Spelt Bread 195
    Sourdough 196–7
buttermilk
    Buttermilk Roast Chicken 89
    Homemade Buttermilk 88
Butternut & Ginger Curd 156

cabbage
    Pickled Red Cabbage 36
canning 10, 11–12, 178
capers
    Shellfish Linguine with Crisp
        Capers 58
carrots
    Piccalilli 138
cauliflower
    Piccalilli 138
celery root
    Piccalilli Rémoulade 139

charcuterie 7
cheese 8
    Apple & Honey Tartlets with Ricotta
        219
    Baked Feta & Shrimp with
        Chermoula 83
    Buffalo Mozzarella & Salami
        Bruschetta with Basil Oil 74
    Butternut & Ginger Curd Ravioli
        with Romano157–8
    Cheese & Cayenne Crackers 193
    Coconut & Lime Baked
        Cheesecake with Pineapple
        in Vanilla Rum 183
    Cornish Blue, Bacon & Caramelized
        Apple Salad 77
    Crisp Manchego with Chorizo-
        Spiked Ratatouille 82
    Dolcelatte Sauce 92
    Goat Cheese & Basil Galettes with
        Cherry Tomato & Thyme Pickles
        143
    Halloumi, Chickpea & Red Onion
        Salad with Pomegranate
        Molasses Dressing 114
    Halloumi, Fig & Almond Salad 86
    Herb & Ricotta Cheesecake with
        Roasted Tomato Pesto 99
    Labneh & Lamb Flatbreads with
        Mint Salsa 79
    Mushroom, Camembert &
        Membrillo Wellingtons 100
    Pea, Bacon & Scamorza Frittatas 137
    Red Onion & Gruyère Focaccia 202
    Rich Homemade Ricotta 218
    Smoked Haddock with Taleggio
        Sauce 96
    Tagliata with Chimichurri
        Sauce 124
    Tartiflette 91
    Twice-Baked Cheese Soufflés with
        Pear & Red Leaf Salad 85
    washed-rind cheese 91
Chermoula 83
cherries
    Cherry & Five-Spice Sauce 168
    Chocolate Risotto with Boozy
        Cherries 186
    Sour Cherry & Pecan Chocolate
        Brownie Cake 207
chestnuts
    Beef, Porcini & Chestnut
        Bourguignon 152

chicken
  Buttermilk Roast Chicken 89
  Chicken Brochettes with Artichoke
    & Oven-Roasted Tomato Confit
    147
  Game, Chicken & Apricot Pie
    18–20
  Lebanese Chicken with Spiced
    Lemon Oil 116
  Moroccan Chicken Patties with
    Date Confit 162
  Paella with Smoked Chicken
    & Shrimp 29
  Pan-Grilled Chicken on Polenta
    with Summer Herb Pesto 118
  Smoked Chicken 28
  Tapenade-Stuffed Chicken 148
chickpeas
  Halloumi, Chickpea & Red Onion
    Salad with Pomegranate
    Molasses Dressing 114
chilies
  Mint Salsa 79
  Sweet Chili Jam 112
  Sweet Chili Mayonnaise 127
  Thai Lemongrass & Chili Oil 108
Chimichurri Sauce 124
chives
  Chive & Lemon Mayonnaise 95
  Summer Herb Pesto 118
chocolate
  Chocolate Risotto with Boozy
    Cherries 186
  Exotic Plum Pudding with Coconut
    & Rum Cream 188
  Ginger & Chocolate Shortbread
    205
  Panforte 213
  Sour Cherry & Pecan Chocolate
    Brownie Cake 207
  Vanilla & White Chocolate Drizzle
    Cakes with Raspberry & Apple
    Jam 210
chorizo
  Chorizo-Spiked Ratatouille 82
  Paella with Smoked Chicken
    & Shrimp 29
  Warm Squid & Chorizo Salad 52
chutneys 10
Cider Sauce 175
cilantro
  Chermoula 83
Citrus Dressing 104

clams
  Smoked Fish & Clam Chowder 55
coconut
  Coconut & Lime Baked
    Cheesecake with Pineapple
    in Vanilla Rum 183
  Fresh Coconut Relish 67
compotes 181
condiments, cupboard 8–10
couscous
  Blackened Fish with Couscous
    & Fresh Coconut Relish 67
  Harissa & Tomato Couscous with
    Lemon-Roasted Vegetables 128
crabmeat
  Crab & Shrimp Cakes with Sweet
    Chili Mayonnaise 127
  Crab Terrine 48
  Creamy Crab Terrine & Scallion
    Tart 49
Cranberry & Pistachio Biscotti 204
cream 8
  Homemade Crème Fraîche 94
  Lemon Curd-Meringue Semifreddo
    177
  Rich Homemade Ricotta 218
cucumber
  Fattoush 116
  Hot Mackerel Niçoise 54
  Roasted Red-Pepper Gazpacho
    with Serrano Chips 134
  Sweet Cucumber Relish 21
curing 7, 64

dairy products 8
dates
  Date Confit 162
  Exotic Plum Pudding with Coconut
    & Rum Cream 188
duck
  Cassoulet with Confit of Duck 33
  Chinese Pancakes with Crisp Duck
    Rillettes 17
  Confit of Duck 32
  Duck & Mango Salad with Citrus
    Dressing 104
  Duck with Cherry & Five-Spice
    Sauce 168
  Duck Rillettes 16
  Polenta Bruschetta with Preserved
    Mushrooms & Smoked Duck 133
  sourcing 17

eggplants
  Chargrilled Eggplant & Skorthalia
    on Crostini 115
  Eggplant Caviar 151
  Harissa & Tomato Couscous with
    Lemon-Roasted Vegetables 128
eggs
  Butternut & Ginger Curd 156
  Crème Pâtissière 216
  Hot Mackerel Niçoise 54
  Lemon Curd-Meringue Semifreddo
    177
  Pea, Bacon & Scamorza Frittatas
    137
  Quail Scotch Eggs 24
  Rhubarb Brûlées 181
  Salad of Smoked Venison,
    Artichokes & Quail Eggs with
    Walnut Oil Dressing 105
  Smoked Haddock with Taleggio
    Sauce 96
equipment 12

Fattoush 116
fennel
  Fennel Carpaccio & Shrimp with
    Marinated Olives 140
fennel seeds
  Garlic & Fennel Mustard 122
figs
  Halloumi, Fig & Almond Salad 86
  Panforte 213
fish 7–8
  Blackened Fish with Couscous
    & Fresh Coconut Relish 67
  curing 64
  Smoked Fish & Clam Chowder 55
  smoking 7–8
  sousing 139
fruit 10
  compotes 181
  French Fruit Tartlets 216
  preserving in alcohol 186
  sauces 168
fruit, dried 213
  Panforte 213

game 7
  choosing 20
  Game, Chicken & Apricot Pie
    18–20

garlic
  Eggplant Caviar 151
  Chimichurri Sauce 124
  Chinese Plum Sauce 121
  Garlic & Fennel Mustard 122
  Garlic & Herb Oil 52
  Garlic–Yogurt Sauce 167
  Skorthalia 115
ginger
  Bacon, Nectarine & Ginger Salad 23
  Butternut & Ginger Curd 156
  Chinese Plum Sauce 121
  Ginger & Chocolate Shortbread 205
guinea fowl
  Roast Guinea Fowl Glazed with
    Orange, Coriander & Thyme
    Jam 172

haddock
  Smoked Fish & Clam Chowder
    55
  Smoked Haddock with Taleggio
    Sauce 96
ham
  Baked Currant- & Clove-Glazed
    Ham 39
  Ham Hock, Roasted Beets & Porcini
    Lentils 26
  jamón Ibérico 7
  Roasted Red-Pepper Gazpacho
    with Serrano Chips 134
Harissa Mayonnaise 128
herbs
  Garlic & Herb Oil 52
  Herb & Ricotta Cheesecake with
    Roasted Tomato Pesto 99
  Lemon & Herb Stuffing 172
  Summer Herb Pesto 118
herring 8

jam 10
jars, canning: sterilizing 11–12

Labneh 78
  Labneh & Lamb Flatbreads with
    Mint Salsa 79
lamb
  Garlic & Fennel Mustard-Crusted
    Leg of Lamb & Pot-Roasted
    Pears 123

Labneh & Lamb Flatbreads with
    Mint Salsa 79
  Lamb, Beet & Puy Lentil Salad with
    Raspberry Vinegar Dressing 165
  Persian Lamb Chops with Eggplant
    Caviar & Beet Chips 151
leeks
  Salmon, Leek & Crème Fraîche
    Braid 95
lemongrass
  Thai Lemongrass & Chili Oil 108
lemons
  Chive & Lemon Mayonnaise 95
  Lemon & Herb Stuffing 172
  Lemon Curd 176
  Preserved Lemon-Stuffed Sardines
    with Garlic–Yogurt Sauce 167
  Preserved Lemons 166
  Spiced Lemon Oil 116
lentils
  Ham Hock, Roasted Beets & Porcini
    Lentils 26
  Lamb, Beet & Puy Lentil Salad with
    Raspberry Vinegar Dressing 165
liver
  Country-Style Pâté 27

mackerel 8
  Hot Mackerel Niçoise 54
  Soused Mackerel with Piccalilli
    Rémoulade 139
mango
  Duck & Mango Salad with Citrus
    Dressing 104
  Exotic Plum Pudding with Coconut
    & Rum Cream 188
Mayonnaise 126
  Chive & Lemon Mayonnaise 95
  Harissa Mayonnaise 128
  Sweet Chili Mayonnaise 127
membrillo 100
Mint Salsa 79
mushrooms
  Beef, Porcini & Chestnut
    Bourguignon 152
  dried 152
  Mushroom & Olive Tapenade 148
  Mushroom, Camembert &
    Membrillo Wellingtons 100
  Mushroom Duxelles 43
  Mushroom Pâté en Croûte with Red
    Onion Relish 159

Polenta Bruschetta with Preserved
    Mushrooms & Smoked Duck 133
  Preserved Mushrooms in Oil 132
  Steak & Ale Potpies 40–2
mustard
  Garlic & Fennel Mustard 122

nectarines
  Bacon, Nectarine & Ginger Salad 23

Oatcakes 192
oils 10
olives
  Hot Mackerel Niçoise 54
  Marinated Olives 140
  Mushroom & Olive Tapenade 148
  White Onion & Sage Farinata with
    Spinach Tzatziki 141
onions
  Creamy Crab Terrine & Scallion
    Tart 49
  Halloumi, Chickpea & Red Onion
    Salad with Pomegranate
    Molasses Dressing 114
  Harissa & Tomato Couscous with
    Lemon-Roasted Vegetables 128
  Pissaladière with Marinated
    Anchovies 47
  Red Onion & Gruyère Focaccia
    202
  Red Onion Relish 159
  White Onion & Sage Farinata with
    Spinach Tzatziki 141
oranges
  Citrus Dressing 104
  Honey-Syrup Topping 206
  Orange & Almond Cake with Honey
    Syrup 206
  Orange, Coriander & Thyme Jam 170
oregano
  Chimichurri Sauce 124
  Summer Herb Pesto 118

Panforte 213
parsley
  Chermoula 83
  Chimichurri Sauce 124
pasta, fresh 158
Pastrami with Sweet Cucumber Relish
  on Rye 21

pastry
    Hot-Water Pastry 18, 40–2
    Pâte Sucrée 216
peaches
    Poached Peaches in Lemongrass
        & Ginger Syrup 178
pears
    Garlic & Fennel Mustard-Crusted
        Leg of Lamb & Pot-Roasted
        Pears 123
    Pear & Red Leaf Salad 85
peas
    Paella with Smoked Chicken &
        Shrimp 29
    Pea, Bacon & Scamorza Frittatas 137
pecans
    Sour Cherry & Pecan Chocolate
        Brownie Cake 207
peppers, bell
    Chorizo-Spiked Ratatouille 82
    Fattoush 116
    Paella with Smoked Chicken
        & Shrimp 29
    Piccalilli 138
    Roasted Red-Pepper Gazpacho
        with Serrano Chips 134
    Seafood & Red Pepper Tagine 153
    Smoky Red-Pepper Ketchup 106
pesto
    Roasted Tomato Pesto 99
    Summer Herb Pesto 118
pH meter 12
pheasant
    Game, Chicken & Apricot Pie
        18–20
Piccalilli 138
    Piccalilli Rémoulade 139
pickles 10–11
pineapple
    Coconut & Lime Baked
        Cheesecake with Pineapple
        in Vanilla Rum 183
    Pineapple in Vanilla Rum 182
Pissaladière with Marinated
    Anchovies 47
pistachios
    Cranberry & Pistachio Biscotti
        204
    Skorthàlia 115
    Spiced Baklava 214
    Summer Herb Pesto 118
plums
    Chinese Plum Sauce 121

polenta
    Pan-Grilled Chicken on Polenta
        with Summer Herb Pesto 118
    Polenta Bruschetta with Preserved
        Mushrooms & Smoked Duck 133
pork 7
    Cassoulet with Confit of Duck 33
    Country-Style Pâté 27
    Glazed Pork Tenderloin in Chinese
        Plum Sauce 121
    Home-Cured Bacon 22
    Slow-Cooked Mexican Pulled Pork
        with Pickled Red Cabbage 36
    Slow-Cooked Pork with Apples
        & Cider Sauce 175
    Slow-Cooked Pork in Milk 90
    Smoky Red-Pepper Pork &
        Zucchini Tzatziki 107
potatoes
    Crab & Shrimp Cakes with Sweet
        Chili Mayonnaise 127
    Hot Mackerel Niçoise 54
    Potato Latkes 71
    Seafood & Red Pepper Tagine 153
    Tartiflette 91
poultry 7
preserving (canning)
    packing jars 11–12
    fruit and vegetables 10–11
preserving kettle 12
Provençal Fougasse 201

quail eggs see eggs

raisins
    Exotic Plum Pudding with Coconut
        & Rum Cream 188
raspberries
    Raspberry, Amaretti & Salted
        Caramel Verrines 189
    Raspberry Vinegar 164
    Simple Raspberry & Apple Jam
        208
relish 11
Rhubarb Brûlées 181
rice
    bomba rice 29
    Chocolate Risotto with Boozy
        Cherries 186
    Paella with Smoked Chicken
        & Shrimp 29

Salmon Gravlax Sushi 57
    Spanish Stuffed Squid 63
salami
    Buffalo Mozzarella & Salami
        Bruschetta with Basil Oil 74
salmon
    Salmon Gravlax with Lemon
        & Ginger 56
    Salmon Gravlax Sushi 57
    Salmon, Leek & Crème Fraîche
        Braid 95
    Vodka-Cured Salmon 64
salsa
    Mint Salsa 79
salt-curing 7
Salted Caramel Sauce 189
sardines
    Preserved Lemon-Stuffed Sardines
        with Garlic–Yogurt Sauce 167
sauces, fruit 168
sausages/sausage meat
    Cassoulet with Confit of Duck 33
    choosing 35
    Merguez Sausages & Smoked
        Paprika Beans 34
    Quail Scotch Eggs 24
    Sausages with Apple & Onion-Seed
        Chutney 35
Sea Bass with Potted Shrimp
    in Butter Sauce 61
Seafood & Red Pepper Tagine 153
shellfish 7
    Shellfish Linguine with Crisp
        Capers 58
    sourcing 58
shrimp
    Baked Feta & Shrimp with
        Chermoula 83
    Fennel Carpaccio & Shrimp
        with Marinated Olives 140
    Crab & Shrimp Cakes with Sweet
        Chili Mayonnaise 127
    Shrimp Fritters with Sweet Chili
        Jam 112
    Paella with Smoked Chicken
        & Shrimp 29
    Potted Shrimp 60
    Sea Bass with Potted Shrimp
        in Butter Sauce 61
    Seafood & Red Pepper Tagine 153
Skorthalia 115
smoking 7–8
    Home-Smoked Trout 68

Smoked Chicken 28
Sourdough 196–7
sousing 139
Spelt Flour 195
spices
    Persian Spice Mix 151
    Za'atar Spice Mix 116
Spinach Tzatziki 141
squid
    Spanish Stuffed Squid 63
    Warm Squid & Chorizo Salad 52
star anise
    Chinese Plum Sauce 121
sterilizing canning jars 11

Tagliata with Chimichurri Sauce 124
Tapenade, Mushroom & Olive 148
thermometer 12
thyme
    Summer Herb Pesto 118
    Sweet Cherry Tomato & Thyme
        Pickles 142
tomatoes
    Artichoke & Oven-Roasted Tomato
        Confit 147
    Chorizo-Spiked Ratatouille 82
    Fattoush 116
    Goat Cheese & Basil Galettes with
        Cherry Tomato & Thyme
        Pickles 143

Harissa & Tomato Couscous with
    Lemon-Roasted Vegetables 128
Hot Mackerel Niçoise 54
Mint Salsa 79
Oven-Roasted Tomatoes 144
Paella with Smoked Chicken
    & Shrimp 29
Roasted Red-Pepper Gazpacho
    with Serrano Chips 134
Roasted Tomato Pesto 99
Steak with Dolcelatte Sauce
    & Balsamic Tomatoes 92
Sweet Cherry Tomato & Thyme
    Pickles 142
Sweet Chili Jam 112
Tagliata with Chimichurri Sauce
    124
trout
    Home-Smoked Trout 68
    Smoked Trout with Potato Latkes
        & Beet Relish 71
tzatziki
    Spinach Tzatziki 141
    Zucchini Tzatziki 107

vanilla 204
    Vanilla & White Chocolate Drizzle
        Cakes with Raspberry & Apple
        Jam 210
vegetables 10–11

venison
    Salad of Smoked Venison,
        Artichokes & Quail Eggs with
        Walnut Oil Dressing 105
    Venison Wellington 43
vinegar 10
    Raspberry Vinegar 164
Vodka-Cured Salmon 64

Walnut Oil Dressing 105

yogurt 8
    Labneh 78
    Spinach Tzatziki 141
    Zucchini Tzatziki 107

Za'atar Spice Mix 116
zucchini
    Chorizo-Spiked Ratatouille 82
    Harissa & Tomato Couscous with
        Lemon-Roasted Vegetables 128
    Pea, Bacon & Scamorza Frittatas
        137
    Shrimp Fritters with Sweet Chili
        Jam 112
    Zucchini Tzatziki 107

ACKNOWLEDGMENTS

AUTHOR ACKNOWLEDGMENTS

The writing of *The Artisan Market* has been a lifelong ambition for me, and would not have been possible without the support and encouragement of Grace Cheetham, Nicola Graimes and the dedicated team at Duncan Baird Publishers. I would also like to thank all our customers for their commitment to and belief in The Bay Tree products—it has been a great journey and an enormous pleasure working with such passionate and enthusiastic foodies over the years. I cannot thank everyone enough for this opportunity, and hope that the book will be enjoyed by many for years to come.

PICTURE ACKNOWLEDGMENTS

Key: t = top, **b** = bottom, **l** = left, **r** = right

Page 2 (tr) Vincenzo Lombardo/Corbis; **2 (bl)** View Pictures/Stockfood; **9** Mario Matassa/Alamy; **14-15** Goran Assner/JohnÈr Images/Corbis; **22** Michael Prince/Corbis; **44-45** ac_bnphotos/Getty Images; **46** idp greek collection/Alamy; **60** nobleIMAGES/Alamy; **72-73** Sandro Vannini/Corbis; **88** Randy Faris/Corbis; **94** Matthiola/Alamy; **102-103** vanda woolsey/Alamy; **122** Vibe Images/Alamy; **130-131** Ocean/Corbis; **132** Tim Pannell/Corbis; **142** Image Source/Getty Images; **156** Diane Macdonald/Alamy; **160-161** Richard Nowitz/National Geographic/Getty Images; **166** Jon Arnold/AWL Images/Getty Images; **176** Jacqui Hurst/Corbis; **190-191** Stefan Braun/Stockfood; **208** Mark Bolton/Garden Picture Library/Getty Images; **218** Image Source/Getty Images.

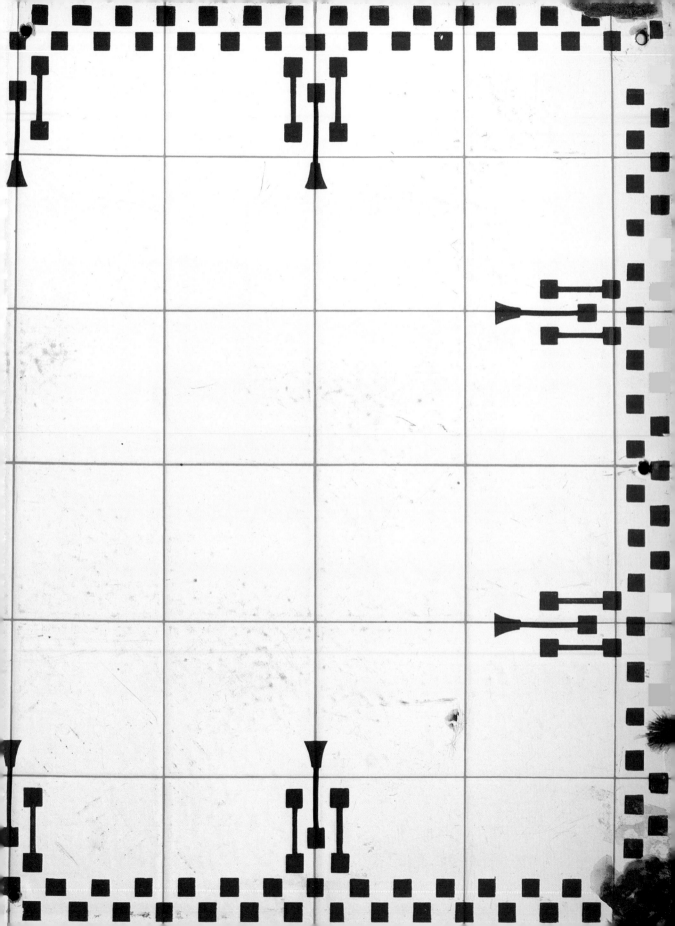

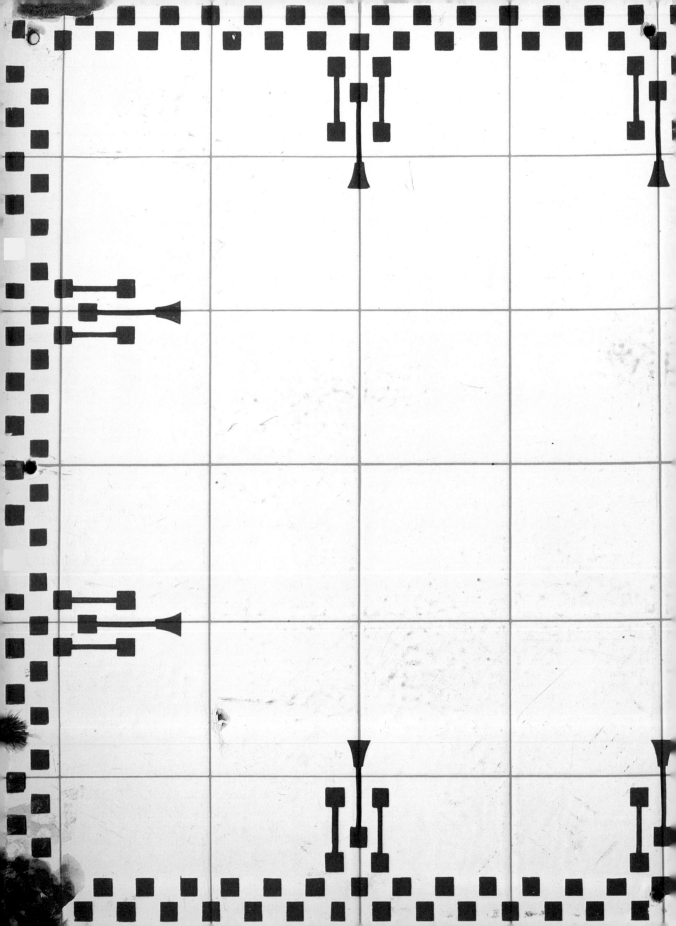